WHAT WOULD YOU DO?

A SERIOUS ANSWER TO A STANDARD QUESTION

JOHN H. YODER

With Joan Baez, Tom Skinner, Leo Tolstoy, and Others

Expanded Edition

HERALD PRESS
Scottdale, Pennsylvania
Waterloo, Ontario

Library of Congress Cataloging in Publication Data
Yoder, John Howard
    What would you do? : a serious answer to a standard question /
John Howard Yoder ; with Joan Baez . . . [et. al.].—Expanded ed.
    p.   cm.
    Includes bibliographical references.
    ISBN 0-8361-3603-9 (alk. paper)
    1. Nonviolence—Religious aspects—Christianity 2. Pacifism—
Religious aspects—Christianity. I. Baez, Joan. II. Title.
BT736.6.Y62   1992
261.8'73—dc20   92-15726
                                                     CIP

The paper used in this publication is recycled and meets the mini-
mum requirements of American National Standard for Information
Sciences—Permanence of Paper for Printed Library Materials,
ANSI Z39.48-1984.

WHAT WOULD YOU DO?
Copyright © 1983, Expanded Edition 1992 by Herald Press,
    Scottdale, Pa. 15683. Published simultaneously in Canada
    by Herald Press, Waterloo, Ont. N2L 6H7. All rights reserved
Library of Congress Catalog Card Number: 92-15726
International Standard Book Number: 0-8361-3603-9
Printed in the United States of America
Cover and book design by David Hiebert and Gwen Stamm

01 99 98 97 96   14 13 12 11 10 9 8

To those in whose defense
I pray I would be ready
To risk my life if need be
But not to kill.

▌Contents

Section 3: But Does It Really Work?

Author's Preface

Section 1 of this book was first written for the scrutiny of my professional colleagues in the academic field of ethics. It was introduced and footnoted with additional details of a logical and technical nature, since that is the business of professionals in ethics as an academic field. Already then, however, the argument referred to concrete cases and to the validation of experience, because that too is data for ethics.

I am grateful to various colleagues, including the leaders of the Mennonite fellowship of Hokkaido, Japan, with whom this outline was first developed in a retreat in Seinen no Ie in October 1968, and Brother Basil O'Leary for the suggestion that the outline of this analysis would be useful for a wider readership. For making it available to readers in the form that appears in this book, I am indebted as well to the assistance of the editors of Herald Press, J. Lorne Peachey, who helped rewrite the material, and to S. David Garber, who assisted in enriching the new edition with more illustrative material. I thank the editor of the *Journal of Religious Ethics*, Dr. James Johnson, and its publisher, the University of Notre Dame Press, for authorization to adapt and republish the material in this form. Readers interested in more argumentative detail about ethics as an intellectual challenge are referred to the original text

(*JRE* 2/2 [1974]: 81-105).

The regularity with which the test case I am discussing is appealed to is reflected in the frequency with which others as well have been drawn to respond to it in ways like my own. I am grateful to those others and their publishers for the authorization to quote them to show that the kind of response I offer here does not stand alone, but speaks for a broad stream or community of similar moral commitment and insight.

The three kinds of material in the separate sections of this book complement one another in important ways. The authors in the second section illustrate that others before me have faced the same challenge and found significant responses to an argument raised by people who seem usually to assume that pacifists had never thought of the question and that it is unanswerable.

The personal experiences in the third section demonstrate concretely that a violent response is not the only or even the most reasonable answer to any and every threat. Thus my more abstract formal analysis in section 1 is linked with similar thinking by other authors in section 2 and with accounts of actual experiences in section 3. The worst-case projection presupposed by the questioner thus finds here responses on three levels, including that of real life.

This expanded edition presents an additional essay by Dale Aukerman at the end of section 2 and articles by Angie O'Gorman, Peggy Faw Gish, Art Gish, and Lawrence Hart at the end of section 3. The list of Christian Peace Resources has also been updated.

                        —*John H. Yoder*
                        Department of Theology
                        University of Notre Dame, 1992

TAKING THE QUESTION SERIOUSLY

Taking the Question Seriously

Sooner or later, in almost any serious discussion about peace and war, someone is sure to ask the standard question: "What would you do if a criminal, say, pulled a gun and threatened to kill your wife" (or daughter or sister or mother, whichever one the challenger decides to use)? It's uncanny how many persons—from seminary professors to draft board members—see this question as a way to test the consistency of the pacifist's convictions that war is wrong.

As we shall see, serious doubt can be raised about whether or not this question fairly represents the issue of war, or whether a pacifist would have to answer it in only one way. But because the question is raised so often, it should—and shall—be answered. Doing so will help illustrate the logic behind the Christian commitment to unwavering, suffering love.

But answering takes care. The reader must be patient with the plodding analysis. That's the only way to move the question from the visceral to the rational level.

I begin by clarifying the nature of the question, looking at some of the assumptions behind it, and testing their validity. From there we'll go on to identify the possible choices one would have, should the "what if. . . .?"

crisis arise. Then we will look at these choices in the light of Christian ethical responsibility. As we go along, we will test whether or not this question applies to the issue of war, as those who pose it assume.

The assumptions behind the question

To deal with the issue, we must bring into the open any unstated assumptions behind the argument. There is no such thing as a simple situation unambiguously dictating a particular line of action. No situation interprets itself. So before we can analyze the "what if. . . ?" we must seek to understand the questioner's assumptions.

1. Determinism

The questioner usually assumes that I alone have a decision to make. My relationship with the other persons in the situation is supposed to be one which unfolds mechanically. The attacker, for example, is preprogrammed to do the worst evil he can—or at least the evil he has fixed his mind on. He is not expected to make any other decisions or act in any other way.

Nor does the question as posed allow for any decisions on the part of the potential victim. I alone am the one making a decision. The assumption is that how I respond solely determines the outcome of the situation.

Later I shall return to this deterministic assumption and compare it to Christian understandings of the person and will of God. At this point two other observations about it are necessary:

a. This mechanical model is unrepresentative of the way decisions are made in war. With all the various parties making interlocking and contradictory decisions about how to act, each impinging on all the others, no one of them can foresee what is sure to happen if one decides this way rather than that. Others are acting at the same time, changing the situation by their actions.

b. Even on the smaller scale of the individual assailant, it is not reasonable to assume that the decisions I make are the only ones being made. There are not simply two preprogrammed tracks on which events can go. Nor am I at any particular point limited to making a choice between them.

Granted, this deterministic assumption is in some sense self-fulfilling. If I tell myself there are no choices, there are less likely to be other choices. Still less will I feel a creative capacity or duty to make them possible if I don't expect them to appear. Thus the limit is then in my mind, not in the situation.

2. Control

The challenge at least assumes my substantial control of the situation, if not my omnipotence. It assumes that if I seek to stop the attacker, I can. Now in some cases this may be true, but in many it is by no means certain. The more serious the threat which an attacker represents, the less likely is it that I will be able to stop him by any means at my disposal.

Relate this to the issue of war. The classic theory of the *just war* includes the criterion of "probable success." It is not reasonable to fight a war which one is sure to lose. In that case, society would suffer both the evil which one inflicts and the evil which one had hoped to prevent. This is a still worse outcome than if one had willingly accepted the evil, however great, which had threatened.

When this criterion is applied to war and revolutionary violence, the reading is striking. Challengers often cite the plot against Adolf Hitler's life in which the well-known Protestant theologian Dietrich Bonhoeffer was implicated. This is supposed to be an example of the need for exceptions to the moral prohibition against violence. Yet Bonhoeffer's effort failed; if it had any effect on the Hitler regime, it was to reinforce its paranoid determination to fight to the last drop of blood. By the criterion of probable success, that attempt was wrong. Yet the people who put the question that way avoid this fact.

The same can be said for the heroic sacrifice of the Colombian priest-sociologist, Camilo Torres. He joined the guerrillas, he explained, as a simple work of love, since it would do away with social oppression. Not only were Torres and his fellow militants killed, but there is no way to measure any positive contribution which their campaign made to their cause.

Failure to be successful is a serious possibility in every case of dramatic confrontation. That is all the more true when both parties to the conflict are acting in unfamiliar roles and under exceptional pressure.

In any war at least one side loses; in some wars, no side wins. On the basis of a calculation of the probability of success, the chances are less than even that I can bring about what I consider a successful result by harming the other party. This is true on the small scale because the attacker is a powerful person or armed for a premeditated offense. It is true on the international level because many dimensions of war cannot be manipulated with certainty even by superior power.

Thus it cannot *generally* be the case that violence is

likely to be successful. Then why label as idealistic those people who have doubts about the successful outcome of the use of violence?

3. Knowledge

The "what if. . . ?" question presupposes, if not omniscience, at least full and reliable information. Not only does it assume on my part that events will unfold in an inevitable way; it also presumes that I am reliably informed about what that unfolding will be like. I know that if I do not kill the aggressor, he will rape my wife, kill my daughter, attack me, or whatever. I also know I will be successful if I try to take his life.

Once again, the reasoning is questionable, even on the individual level. The outcome of any kind of combat is unpredictable. Even more is this true on the international level. When military planners use hypothetical circumstances, any such scenario makes untested, unverifiable assumptions about the psychology of the enemy. Consider the American military think tank that works through how Russians or Chinese will react to a variety of nuclear situations. That think tank must claim exact knowledge of how any reasonable Russian or Chinese leader will respond to such a threat. Yet although such guesses can be entered into the computer with great apparent detail and precision, no one can predict with certainty how anyone would really react to an absolutely unprecedented crisis.

As soon as a situation exists in which several persons are making decisions at the same time—all acting on the basis of what they think the others think and all at least partly trying to deceive the others—we can be quite sure of one thing: No one has sure knowledge of what

will happen. Certainly anyone whose vision of conflict
is deeper than that of the television western has some
awareness of the complexity of situations and some no-
tion of how seldom things turn out the way predicted.
That is especially true when people predict positive
results coming about through the use of violence.

4. Individualism

The question as usually posed assumes that the decision and what happens are individual matters. Not only
does this make the "What if. . . .?" situation quite unrepresentative of the social and institutional dimensions of war; it even makes it untrue for any particular
concrete case.

The person who is being attacked (my wife or mother
or daughter) is also a responsible being and should be
part of my decision-making process. If this person
shares my values, then she would be guided by some of
the same considerations which guide me. It would
certainly be improper for me as a third party in the conflict to deal with her enemy in a way she would not
desire. At least some Christian women would not want
to be protected by lethal violence.

5. Righteousness

The logic of this approach assumes my righteousness.
Not only am I able to calculate what would bring about
the best outcome. I also assume that I am morally
qualified to be judge, jury, and executioner—and to
perform all those roles in one second. It is taken for
granted that I have all it takes to be honest about this
hard decision, even when it involves weighing my own
welfare and interests against those of another.

This shorting out of critical objectivity may be the most improper of all the assumptions. We know that most times individuals do not have full objectivity. When we move to the group or the nation, there is even less reason to assume that a center of power is capable of standing in judgment on its own selfish temptations. As Reinhold Niebuhr pointed out, it is less possible for a group to be consistently unselfish than for an individual. The danger of being one-sided is increased precisely where power is greatest and when capacity for self-criticism is least.

6. *Alternatives*

The threat to my interests is put by the "what if. . . ?" question in a way that excludes the possibility that the other party might have reasons for behaving in the way I perceive to be wrong. There is no room for the possibility that the offender might be a Jean Valjean, only looking for bread for his hungry children in the home of someone who has more bread than needed. Nor is there room for the possibility that the offender might be an oppressed person (as in the theories of Frantz Fanon), whose human dignity is dependent upon his rising and destroying a symbol of oppressive order (an innocent symbol, true, but that makes no difference for the psychic need of the former slave).

The emotional twist to the question

If the situation of attacker and person being attacked stayed on the rational level, it would be much easier to debate and answer logically. But the way the question is put does not allow us to do that. It appeals to family connections and bonds of love so that it becomes a problem of emotions as well as thought. Instead of discussing what is generally right or wrong, it personalizes the situation by making it an extension of my own self-defense and by involving elements of social disorder and sexual menace.

There's also the appeal to my view of who I am. The unspoken suggestion is that if I do not respond to the brutal threat in a brutal way, I will not be a man. It reminds me that I often do not live up to my principles. These emotional overtones are irrelevant to the discussion of the conditions under which it is morally justified in principle to take life, yet the question as put makes the most of them.

Not only is this stock case one in which an emotional appeal is made to my virility as the defender of those entrusted to me; it also tends to be a sexist argument. It assumes the potential victim is a dependent being, a woman, one who needs protection by a stronger male. She who is prey participates only as an object. What would happen to the hypothetical argument if the assailant was a woman and the victim a man?

For the purposes of the argument, I leave the challenge in its traditional gender-specific form, but not without registering objection to its sexist tilt. Within this setting, it is harder to sustain the moral challenge for the male to renounce violence; but if we can do that, the question should also be settled for other situations.

Especially is this emotional dimension of the question more visible when the discussion centers on one's duty to protect someone *else*. Often the questioner will heighten this aspect of the argument by saying, "Perhaps as a Christian you do have the right to sacrifice your own welfare to be loving toward an attacker. But do you have the right to sacrifice the welfare of others for whom you are responsible?"

We must pierce through the screen of this apparent altruism and point out that it distorts the real nature of the argument. It is an altruistic form of egoism when I defend *my* wife or *my* child because they are precisely *my own.* This argument does not suggest that I would have the same responsibility to defend the wives and children of Vietnamese, for example, who are being attacked by my countrymen. It does not suggest any special concern for the wife or child of the attacker. The reason I should defend my wife and child in this argument is not that they are my *neighbors,* innocent threatened third parties, but because they are *mine.* Thus this becomes an act of selfishness; though covered over with the halo of service to others, it is still self-oriented in its structure.

Now self-centeredness is not all bad; "thou shall not seek thy own interest" is not a generally accepted moral axiom. In fact, one can argue that a certain amount of self-love is necessary for psychological health and to motivate one to take care of what has been entrusted to oneself. But if I make self-centeredness or egotism the basis on which I choose how to respond in any situation, that is not a Christian approach to a problem. Christianity relativizes the value of self and survival as it affirms the dignity of the enemy and offender. True, the potential victim is my neighbor and thus deserving of my help. But the attacker also at that moment becomes a neighbor. It is also a form of egoism to make any attempt to distinguish between these two and say that the nearness of my family member as preferred neighbor takes precedence over that of my attacker. Again, this

cannot be a sufficient basis for Christian ethical decision-making.

War is different

We have already considered some serious points
where the analogy between self-defense and war
breaks down. We need to examine more of these. Even
if I could agree that it might be my Christian duty to
defend my family against an attacker by killing, the fact
that the analogy between the two does not hold means I
could still with complete consistency reject all war.

In the case of the individual attacker, it is the guilty
person who would be the target of my defensive violence. I would not run serious risk of harming innocent
bystanders. Even less would I go to my attacker's home
to destroy his family.

But that does happen in modern war. Most of those
who suffer are not the attackers or the aggressors (who
these would be in a nuclear attack would likely not be
clear). In fact, the airman or missileman who is actively
attacking, like the top statesman or the general who
made the decisions to attack, is less likely to be harmed
than most categories of civilians in the line of fire.

The Vietnam conflict illustrated this discrepancy
between the individual facing an attacker and what
happens in modern warfare. Part of the argument for
that war was to keep Americans from needing to defend
themselves "on the beaches of California." The Vietnamese tragedy—even the very fact that "we" chose to
"defend" the South against the North—became a matter of using Vietnam as a place to fight China. To be
logical and fair, the image of the invader must be turned
around. It was the American forces which were enter-

ing someone else's homeland on the grounds that their neighbors might attack us in the future. A comparison on the individual level would be a man entering my house to fight my wife because he fears my neighbor might sometime want to attack his home.

Another difference between war and the situation calling for self-defense is that of jurisdiction. In the case of personal threat, the attacker and the victim and I all live in the same legally organized community, subject to the same legislation. We all know (including the attacker) that he is committing a crime, as defined by the laws of the state, and that if apprehended he would be liable for punishment. If I then act in self-defense, in the place of the absent policeman, that defensive action is subject to review by the police or the courts. It will only be justified by them if I can demonstrate the nature and the certainty of the threat.

None of this applies in the same simple way to war. Here there is not such a clear definition of what constitutes aggression or what is innocence. There is usually no higher court to decide whether what was claimed as legitimate defense actually was that. There is no regular procedure of review to determine whether a nation exceeded the legitimate use of preventive force.

Then there is the question of authority. In the situation of self-defense, the victim would clearly be in my own home, with no question of my "legitimate authority" to defend. In war the aggression is rarely so clean-cut, and the defense seldom stays on its home terrain.

The analogy also breaks down on the matter of preparation. Defending my home demands a minimum of this; it suffices to have a weapon. War, however, is unthinkable unless a nation has been making costly

preparations for years. Having a gun in my house, if the
neighbors know about it, *might* be a deterrent to their
efforts to break in (although it also increases other risks
to my family), but piling up armaments tends to increase rather than decrease international tensions.

The development of contingency plans makes possible types of military operations which otherwise could
not occur. I could have a pistol in my drawer for use
only as a last resort (although, in fact, handguns kept at
home are used more often against family members than
against intruders). But when that last resort is institutionalized on an international scale, it becomes just
one more increment on the preplanned escalation of
usable "instruments of politics."

The difference between war and self-defense is apparent when we consider how decisions are made.
When the question, "What would you do if . . . ?" is put
to an individual, a decision must be made at a given
time and place. In war, however, even the head of a
government does not make a free decision at one particular instant for or against conflict. The dimensions of
emotional pressure, split-second decisiveness, and
unique momentary risk which characterize the hypothetical case—some of them tending to push toward jus-
tifying the killing of the individual offender—are not at
all representative of war.

It is possible that having a gun in the house might not
completely change the atmosphere of our family
relationship, but it has been demonstrated that turning
a national economy over to the military-industrial-
communications-surveillance complex necessary to
gear up for war does bring about a great change in the
character of the nation's life. The very effort to defend

"freedom" (i.e., national sovereignty) generally entails a real sacrifice of freedom.

There is another difference between the individual threat and war. If I kill the person menacing my family, escalation is relatively unlikely. But in war, escalation is practically unavoidable. There has never been a major war which did not take on greater dimensions of destructiveness as it continued than were projected by those who began it. Any moral consideration must take into account what one stands to lose through violent defense compared to what one claims to defend. In the case of war, the costs are always more than the advocates of war calculate them to be at the outset.

A final way the analogy breaks down is in the matter of guilt and innocence. The attacker in the "what if . . . ?" situation is clearly and solely the guilty one. His brutality may well be partly the product of his environment (and views will differ as to whether this makes him morally less to blame), but he is clearly the aggressor, without right for his attack. In war the isolated single act of unjust brutal attack is especially difficult to find. All sober political thought warns us to avoid the "devil" and "ruffian" theories of international conflict.

At this point there comes to the surface much of the drama and some of the confusion of the unending debate about pacifism as a social stance and as a personal discipleship—and the link between the two. There is no convincing analogy between war and personal self-defense. Mohandas Gandhi and Thomas Merton, for example, were ready without embarrassment to acknowledge the legitimacy of the violent defense of one's immediate family or self, without seeing this as any compromise to their rejection of all organized violence in social or national causes.

Leo Tolstoy showed how the two situations were completely different in his answer to the "what if . . . ?" question put to him by William Jennings Bryan. Tolstoy replied that in all his seventy-five years he had never met anywhere the fantastic hypothetical brigand who would murder or outrage a child before his eyes, whereas in war millions of brigands kill with complete license. "When I said this," Tolstoy reported, "my dear companion, with his characteristically quick understanding, did not let me finish, laughed, and agreed that my argument was satisfactory."

My willingness to accept the stock argument for purposes of clarification must never lead us to forget that it radically misrepresents what is really going on in the institutionalization of social coercion. The test case as posed not only differs from war. It also does violence to concern for general social responsibility. If in order to be able to protect my loved ones, I should have a gun in the house, what then does it do to a society for every household to have a gun? Will there be fewer crimes in a society in which every citizen is prepared to take the law into one's own hands?

The options available

So much for consideration of the assumptions behind the "what if . . . ?" question. We come now to the decision itself. How do we answer the question?

We must note, first of all, that the questioner wants us simply to answer either yes or no. For most questioners, the only choices which the question offers are defense

---

°Ernest J. Simmons, *Leo Tolstoy* (Boston: Little, Brown, 1946), 623.

—which must necessarily be lethal—and non-defense, which is sure to permit the worst to happen.

But this is a wildly illogical way to pose the problem. There are certainly several more possible kinds of outcomes. We prejudice the argument if we set up the discussion as if there were only two possible outcomes.

What are these various options?

1. Tragedy

One possibility is unmitigated tragedy. The attacker is able to carry out his evil designs. In most people's minds, this would be pure catastrophe, an evil which God would not want to permit, an event which forever after will be looked on with horror. The critic of the pacifist position assumes that such tragedy must be excluded at all necessary cost and is sure to happen unless someone interferes with the actions of the attacker.

2. Martyrdom

Another serious possibility in a situation of menace is martyrdom. Some suffering, though recognized as evil, has its place in God's saving purposes. In any case, we are all going to die sometime, and so are our loved ones. It is irrational to look at this problem as if innocent death were in all situations at all costs absolutely to be avoided.

Throughout history there have been many instances of the deaths of Christian believers because they behaved in a Christian way in the face of the agents of evil. With time these have come to be seen as important and even representative of the true character of the church. The deaths of such Christian disciples make a greater contribution to the cause of God and to the welfare of the world than they would have made if they had stayed alive at the cost of killing. For ever after, they are remembered with respect.

Nor does the consideration of martyrdom inject into the discussion sectarian, irrational, emotional, or illegitimately religious considerations. Marxism, nationalist movements, and the civil rights movement have their martyrs as well. Communism has its Rosa Luxemburg, Castrosim its Che, Americanism its Custer and its Alamo.

a. The victim as martyr. If it should happen that an attack befalls someone when no defender is around, many would speak of such an innocent death as more than the effect of mindless hazard. Others would judge such suffering to be pointless tragedy, or even a proof of the nonexistence of God, or the senseless evil nature of reality. But for others, such slaughter would bring about a renewed commitment to work for the kind of world in which such things do not happen. The tragedy thus turns into martyrdom.

b. The defender as martyr. But the more congruent application of meaningful sacrifice would be for me to intervene in such a way that, without my destroying the aggressor, he would refocus his attack upon me instead of upon the originally intended victim. To risk one's own life to save that of another is a kind of heroism which most people see as fitting when the danger comes from a fire, a natural disaster, a runaway vehicle, or a military enemy. So why then should not my risking myself to give the victim a chance to escape be the first logical alternative to the "what if . . . ?" question? After all, death is not the greatest evil one can suffer. A believer's death can relate to God's will and be part of his victory over evil in this world.

3. Another way out

Any honest contemplation of the future must admit uncertainty. Never are there only two choices. For this reason, an unforeseen happy outcome cannot be *logically* excluded. We can logically consider two ways this might happen.

a. The natural way out. When I see a person about to attack my mother or daughter or wife, I might think of some way to disarm the attacker emotionally. It might be a loving gesture, a display of moral authority, or my undefensive harmlessness which would disarm him psychologically. I might use nonlethal force or a ruse. If money is part of what he wants, I could hand it over. I might interpose myself and let the intended victim escape.

Such solutions are reported with striking frequency throughout religious biographical literature. They have been found in tight spots in the past. It stands to reason that such options are more likely to be looked for—and thus more likely to be found—if the defender is not trigger-happy, still more likely if he is not even armed, and even still more likely if he believes in an intervening God.

However, I am less likely to look for another way out if I have told myself beforehand that there can be none or if I have made advance provision for an easy brutal defense. I am more likely to find a creative way out if I have already forbidden myself the easy violent answer.

I am still more likely to find it if I have disciplined my impulsiveness and fostered my creativity by the study and practice of a nonviolent lifestyle, or of Aiki-Do, the nonviolent variant of the martial arts.

The possibility of such unforeseen, creative, or coincidental deliverances is not limited to those who would interpret them in Christian terms. Nonlethal violence, ruse, or the disarming gesture of unexpected respect are possible for anyone.

b. The providential way out. The options I've outlined above and below are theologically neutral. But there is an option which is distinctly theistic, if not uniquely Christian—what we have traditionally referred to as "providential" escape. Whatever the modern mind may think of the category of miracle, it has had an undeniable place in the history of Christian thinking about how to look at the future.

We cannot be sure what the apostle Paul meant by assuring his readers (1 Cor. 10:13) that with whatever testing they might face, God would provide a "way of escape" (RSV), "the way out" (NRSV). Certainly all biblical faith and Christian consensus until recently has affirmed a providential direction of the affairs of humans toward that end which is described as "good for those who love God" (Rom. 8:28, NRSV).

Since providential deliverance is not predictable, it is impossible to say from a scientific or historical perspective whether this category is really distinguishable from the "natural" "way out" (3-a). That kind of saving outcome combines coincidence and imagination to produce a result which, although unforeseeable, can be explained after the fact. We cannot address here the philosophical problem of whether or not the Christian concept of Providence or miracle is dependent on our not being able to explain a saving event after the fact. Yet there is the classical Christian way of regarding one's future to be in the hands of God. This can provide logical grounds for being freed from the assumption that in the face of a threat, there are only two options, both lethal, which need to be considered.

4. Attempted killing

This is the other possibility, alongside option 1 (tragedy), which the usual argument takes seriously. It can lead to one of two outcomes.

a. Successful. As defender I may succeed in killing the attacker. I would do this on my own authority, but I would do so with the confidence that it is done in the name of a higher moral authority, which commends or demands the defense of the innocent. Legally I would trust that my action could be seen as the exercise of emergency powers vested in every citizen by common law. The one who asks the "what if . . . ?" question assumes this will be easy to do.

b. Unsuccessful. But logically there is another possibility: I might fail to kill. In this way I add another evil to an evil already present, and we suffer them both. This is then the greatest evil: that I might seek to defend the innocent but fail to do so and only make matters worse.

If the aggressor has superior force (likely, since he was prepared for the attack), if he has the unthinking drive of the perverted spirit which will not stop for fear or pain (also likely, if he is as inaccessible to reason as the stock argument assumes), or if he is a better shot than I, then my efforts to stop him with his kind of weapon may only make the matter worse. This will cause greater suffering than the option of tragedy. Not only will the victim likely be killed, but so will I, the defender. In his anger the attacker may turn on more persons than if he had not been opposed and further enraged.

Thus the "what if . . . ?" question has more than the two commonly conceived possible options. We have noted seven:

1. *Tragedy*   3. *Another way out*
                             a. Natural
2. *Martyrdom*   b. Providential
   a. Victim
   b. Defender   4. *Attempted killing*
                             a. Successful
                             b. Unsuccessful

These can be ranked as to desirability. Option 4-a (successful killing) is an evil; it ends a life and deprives the attacker of any chance of repentance or growth. Option 1 (tragedy) is obviously more evil in the mind of the questioner, who would use 4-a to prevent 1. But option 4-b (unsuccessful killing) is still worse, for it brings together two evil outcomes.

The four other options (2-a, 2-b, 3-a, 3-b) represent "saving" or "happy" outcomes. We need not weigh them exactly in terms of desirability or probability but only note that they are all morally positive in contrast with the other three.

In evaluating these options it soon becomes evident

that by exercising option number 4, I close the door to the possible saving solutions (2 or 3). None of those can happen if I choose to kill. Does this also mean I do not trust God to work things out (2-a, 2-b, 3-b)? Does it also mean I do not trust myself to be courageous or creative enough to find another way (3-a)?

To renounce killing (4-a), on the other hand, is the path of trust and faith. It leaves open the possibility for Providence (3-b) or martyrdom (2). It is not lazy; it faces the challenge of creating another way (3-a). It is responsible, for it prevents the worst (4-b).

Let us move out of the emotionally colored common description of this dramatic encounter and think soberly about the choices it offers. We now see how logically preposterous it is to assume, as does the questioner, that there are only two possible outcomes (1 and 4-a). There are many more. We have no way to judge before the event how *probable* each of these outcomes would be; but no one can deny that they are all logically *possible*, and some preferable to others.

If I choose 4-a as the way out, then I don't trust in the imagined course of events, or in the providence of God. Instead, right there in the emotionally loaded situation, I give myself authority to choose that option that is sure to be destructive. By doing so, I close the door on all other alternatives, at least two or three of which could be saving. I do this on the grounds that there is one other outcome (option 1) which would be more harmful to my own loved one than the other destructive alternative. By assuming it is my business to prevent evil or bring judgment upon it, I authorize myself to close the door on possibilities of reconciliation and healing. When I take it into my hands to guarantee that events will not turn out in a way painful or disadvantageous to me, I close off possibilities of reconciliation which might have been let loose in the world.

A second look at another way out

But is "another way out," whether by nature or by Providence, really an option in the world in which we live? Does it hold up as a genuine alternative in a society which values scientific explanation and observable phenomena? Because the modern mind asks that question, and many belittle the possibility of another way out, we need to take a closer look at this option for dealing with the "what if . . . ?" question. In other words, does it really work that way?

The data is impressive. At the center of the Hebrew Scriptures lies the recitation of those mighty deeds where YHWH/Adonai saved those who trusted him. As these events happened, they were not able to manipulate the fulfillment of YHWH/Adonai's promise through their own wisdom or strength.

The annals of Christian history are also full of such unhoped-for deliverances. A. Ruth Fry, a British Quaker, gathered scores of anecdotes from many centuries and many faiths which showed the workings of another way out. Included in her 1939 volume, *Victories Without Violence,* ° are accounts of various persons who were able to face a threatening situation and overcome evil and destruction with little or no force on their part. Other examples follow, in section 3, on pages 87-141.

It is striking that expectation of such deliverance,

° A. Ruth Fry, *Victories Without Violence,* reprinted in Liberty Literary Works, no. 1 (Santa Fe: Ocean Tree Books, 1986).

together with the assumption that it would be wrong to resort to violence, crops up repeatedly, especially in Christian missionary biography. These reports have even come from settings where there had been no explicit thought or traditional teaching about pacifism or nonresistance. The stories show that such a response seems to rise naturally out of a religious perception of the world and of oneself as being in the hand of God. It is not a forced product of a rigid principle of nonviolence.

One testimony to this kind of creative confidence in the way out is the voice of Johannel Hamel, pastor in Communist East Germany. His struggle was with the issue of truth and falsehood, not with violence. Yet his approach is just as logically applicable to the question of killing because of the way he puts the problem of calculating versus uncalculating obedience, of closed system versus open history.

Shall a Christian in a Communist land make an issue of honesty and faith? Hamel asks. Should one in such a setting lie low and seem to accept the system and its injustices? Hamel finds an answer in the analogy of God "making room" or "opening doors" as the believer walks obediently a step at a time:

> Time and again God creates loopholes, so to speak, open space in the midst of closed systems of unbelief and hatred of God. Here the possibility is offered and realized for doing the good, reasonable, and well-pleasing, although these systems theoretically seem to leave no room for such action.

°Johannel Hamel, *How to Serve God in a Marxist Land* (New York: Association Press, 1959), 98f.

Where people take their place in this self-movement of the Gospel, there opens, usually by surprise, a door by which they can get on in their earthly life. To be sure most of the time this door is only visible in the last moment. One must have *enough faith to run against a door-less wall up to the last centimeter,* in the certain hope that God who leads one in this way will not allow his people to break their heads. . . . More than once we have believed ourselves to be finished. . . . Then in the last minute God stepped in and made it clear to us, so clear that we were ashamed of ourselves, so that he only needs to move a little finger to make things come out quite otherwise than we could have foreseen.[*]

That is not speculative, logical, ethical theory; it is testimony with living experience to illustrate it.

The Christian understanding of divine Providence is not only that it might sometimes provide a "way of escape." It is also that Christians are called to testify to such a vision of God's care and to trust in it. This is necessary for any meaningful understanding of prayer.

To elect option 4-a (successful killing) denies the faith. Then we assume that there are no unforeseen creative alternatives and no divine possibilities available. Suppose I justify a choice limited to one of two most undesirable outcomes which can be foreseen, and choose the one which I feel would be least undesirable to me and mine. But that in effect says that God has no redemptive intention in this situation. Or I assume that if God has such an interest, I am his only tool for bringing it about, which I can do only by imposing my own choice of what I consider the lesser evil.

Yet Christian belief in resurrection does not simply

---

[*]Johannel Hamel, *A Christian in East Germany* (New York: Association Press, 1960), 26f., with italics added.

refer to one bygone event but also to resurrection as God's pattern of action in human experience. Does this belief not mean that God might demonstrate his saving intent exactly where we do not see how a situation can possibly be worked out? Precisely because God is the one who must act, I cannot say how that might be. But I can be sure that it is of little help to God if I try to settle the matter on my own in a destructive way.

In classical Christian thought, *Providence* designates the conviction that the events of history are under God's control. This manifests itself in ways beyond both our discerning and our manipulating. Their pattern may occasionally be perceived by the prophet, and later they will be celebrated by the community.

The sources I've cited so far are Christian. Yet it should not be thought that only Christians, or only adherents of the three Abrahamic faiths, show evidence of some kind of trust in Providence. The Marxist confidence in the dialectic of history, the democrat's trust in the *vox populi*, the radical's trust in "the revolution," or the Oriental's logic of noncontradiction and mistrust of visible evidence—all these can and do lead to ways out of difficult situations that go beyond what can be foreseen or predicted.

We are not concerned with trying to verify any of these reports of divine intervention. Yet those who have gone through such experiences conclude for themselves that there was a way out which they did not foresee. Thus there have been saving events as perceived exceptions to the predictability of the fulfillment of the evil design of an aggressor—not just once, but several or many times, believers would say. Logically, one may never therefore exclude such a possibility.

So when the threat of destructive aggression *seems* to leave us no outcome but defensive violence, the possibility of a less-violent outcome is always there—at least logically or potentially. Until it has been tested, it cannot be said that the "what if . . . ?" situation as put by our questioner has taken this into account. This does not mean that we can predict how many times the less-violent way out will be found. That depends on many variables, including the extent of my trust that it might be available. But that possibility is always there if it is ever the case that conflict can have an outcome so that after the fact one says, "Shooting him was not the best option." The "what if . . . ?" situation has been hypothetically constructed to predispose a particular outcome. Joan Baez puts it this way: "If you have a choice between a real evil and a hypothetical evil, always take the hypothetical one." Dale Brown argues in the same mood, claiming the right to add hypothetical detail (see both arguments in section 2).

I am less inclined than Baez and Brown to insist on challenging the logic of the question with hypothetical counter-cases. One can come to the same conclusion as I have done by taking the stock question seriously. But the point Baez and Brown make is valid: The hypothetical definition of specific situations may properly be challenged by asking for greater precision in detail. That challenge is one of the ways to note that situations are more hopeful than they initially seem.

Leo Tolstoy rephrases the same point: "Why should a non-Christian . . . decide to kill the criminal in order to defend the child? By killing the former he kills for certain; whereas he cannot know positively whether the criminal would have killed the child or not."

More specific Christian dimensions

So far I've been answering the "what if . . . ?" question on the basis of logic. I've addressed the hypothetical test of how consistent one could be in meeting a conflict situation. With the exception of noting the possibility of divine intervention in human affairs (option 3-b), nothing has been said about the other aspects of Christian belief which make the deterministic claim (dilemma 1 or 4-a) even more inadequate.

There are such perspectives of Christian faith which expose the spiritual poverty of thinking only of two options: kill or be killed. I've avoided them until now, but not because Christian commitment is an appendix to be added after all the important analysis is done. I did not want to give room for the misunderstanding that Christians simply call in the transcendent dimension to avoid realism in dealing with life as it is.

I have also meant to show that there is nothing irrational about Jesus' way of facing conflict. But it is not on that basis that I accept it, nor on the basis that one can make a case for it on other grounds. Neither is my acceptance of Jesus' way founded in the confidence that, if you really put your mind to it, you can be reassured that there might be at least a fighting chance of a safe way through the brutal encounter. I accept Jesus' way because I confess that Jesus is Lord.

So the Christian's answer to "What would you do if . . . ?" is not, "I would work creatively at 3-a and pray for 3-b and be willing in the crunch to settle for 2." That is the legalist's logical answer. The Christian faith has additional dimensions which enter into confronting this stock, hypothetical situation:

1. Christian love of the enemy goes beyond the bounds of decent humanism.

Any respectable person will try to treat one's neighbor as one wishes to be treated oneself. This is true simply out of reciprocal self-interest. It is also part of one's self-respect to discipline oneself by this standard and thus rise above the level of simple retaliation.

But Jesus goes well beyond this kind of moral superiority. In his own life and career and in his instructions to his disciples, the enemy becomes a privileged object of love. We confess that the God who has worked out our reconciliation in Christ is a God who loves his enemies at the cost of his own suffering. Hence, we are to love our enemies beyond the extent of our capacity to be a good influence on them or to call forth a reciprocal love from them. In other ethical systems, the "neighbor" may well be dealt with as an object of our obligation to love. But Jesus goes further and makes of our relation to the adversary the special test of whether the love we have is derived from the love of God.

This is counter to the general assumption that Jesus simply restated the law's command to "love your neighbor as yourself" (Lev. 19:13, cited by Jesus in Mt. 22:40 and Mk. 12:28ff.). Instead, Jesus' "new commandment" was that his disciples should love as he loved—or as God loved them. "Love your neighbor as yourself" is the center not of Jesus' teaching but of the law which he fulfills and transcends.

So the answer for the Christian to the "what if . . . ?" question is this: I seek to deal with the aggressor as God in Christ has dealt with me—or as I would wish to be dealt with. The capacity for this simple act is not dependent on being able to "put one's mind to it" and think through the options. In fact, thinking through the options may make obedience harder. The simple, loving Christian may never have thought through the situation but still responds out of God's love for oneself. Such a believer may well be nearer to obedience than those of us who think we must logically process the kinds of concerns about which I have just written.

2. The Christian's loyalty to the bonds of social unity is loosened by the decision to follow Christ.

In various statements recorded in the Gospels, Jesus called his disciples to forsake not only houses and land but even father and mother, spouse and child. Any consideration of what this means must at least make us question the assumption that the first test of moral responsibility or of virility is the readiness to kill in defense of one's family.

The great Luther hymn "A Mighty Fortress" states this, in English translation: "Let goods and kindred go; this mortal life also." The German is more dramatic: "They seize wife and child; let it take its course!" This is not mere poetic exaggeration. Martin Luther taught nonresistance on the personal level. He believed that violence was permissible only at the behest of a legitimate government in a just cause.

3. The Christian's understanding of the resurrection of the dead, of heaven and hell, and of eternal life—all this informs the approach to the "what if . . . ?" situation.

We've already conceded that the classic Christian understanding of Providence might not be accepted by modern debaters. The same is true of classical Christian understandings of a transcendent life. We cannot impose such conceptions upon modern challengers. Yet at least we can ask those within historic Christianity to understand that our beliefs may reinforce our readiness to accept the cost of obedience when confronted by a hostile aggressor.

Consider the belief that there is such a thing as hell, some kind of extension or reaffirmation beyond death of the meaning of life, in which one's fate or state is conditioned by the self-centered, shallow kind of life one has been leading. I can ask my challenger to acknowledge that on the basis of such a belief, it would be most likely that my killing the attacker would seal for him that negative destiny. I would take away from him any possibility of repentance and faith. I would be doing this in order to save from death someone who—pardon the piety, but it is a meaningful Christian stance—is "ready to meet her Maker." To keep out of heaven temporarily someone who wants to go there ultimately anyway, I would consign to hell immediately someone whom I am in the world to save.

4. Committed Christians see in their life of faith not merely an ethical stance in which they want to be consistent, nor a set of rules they want to be sure not to break, but a gracious privilege which they want to share.

They guide their lives not so much by "How can I avoid doing wrong?" or even "How can I do the right?" as by "How can I be a reconciling presence in the life of my neighbor?" From this perspective, I might justify firm nonviolent restraint, but certainly never killing. Most of the time the committed Christian testifies, at least in theory, that God intervenes in the lives of selfish creatures to change those lives, and that he does so through his children. When is that testimony tested more than when I am invited to act toward an aggressor as though there can be for him no change of heart?

5. *For the Christian, to bear the martyr's cross is to share in God's way with his world.*

The New Testament and much later Christian testimony indicate that martyrdom is in some sense a normal path which at least some Christians need to follow at least sometimes. How then could I possibly be led along the path of innocent suffering if my pragmatic managing of the "what if . . . ?" situation determines this as the one thing that I must not let happen?

6. *Christian faith warns me that I tend to use self-centered control of my decision as a tool of rebelliousness, to solidify my independence from my Maker.*

We've already noted the moral limits of a self-centered decision-making process. But Christian faith goes much further. Common sense tells us that people tend to be selfish and allow their selfishness to influence their perception. Christian thought goes on to label as "pride" that rebellious autonomy on which I insist despite the fact that ultimately, if not overcome by God's grace, it means my own destruction.

Common sense says that any person is limited in the capacity to observe and evaluate the facts by a particular point of view and the limits of vision. But Christian faith tells me, in addition, that my selfish mind, my impatient and retaliating spirit, and my adrenalin—these all positively warp the way I perceive the facts to make them reflect my self-esteem and my desire to be independent of my Creator at the cost of my neighbor. Thus common sense argues for modesty about my capacity to make valid decisions by myself. However, the Christian understanding of sin goes well beyond that to call me to repent of the very idea that I might make a decision completely on my own.

The real temptation of "good" people like us is not the crude, the crass, and the carnal. The really refined temptation, with which Jesus himself was tried, is that of egocentric altruism. It is to claim oneself to be the incarnation of a good and righteous cause for which others may rightly be made to suffer. It is stating one's self-justification in the form of a duty to others.

Finally, I do not know what I *would* do if some insane or criminal person were to attack my wife or child, sister or mother. But I know that what I *should* do would be illuminated by what God my Father did when his "only begotten Son" was being threatened. Or by what Abraham, my father in the faith, was ready to sacrifice out of obedience; he was ready to give up his son because he believed in the resurrection (Heb. 11:17-19). Jesus himself "endured the cross" "for the sake of the joy . . . set before him" (Heb. 12:2, NRSV).

I ponder my own readiness to accept that kind of love as my duty and privilege. Such readiness does not arise from contemplation of my moral strength but in confession of the nature of the God who has revealed himself in Jesus Christ. It is not based on a craving for heroism, self-confidence, pious enthusiasm, or masochism. Instead, my calling to respond to a threat with sacrificial love is founded in a confession: the Jesus who gave his life at our hands is at one and the same time the revelation of that true humanity which is God's instrument in the world.

OTHER WAYS TO RESPOND

The way I have answered the "what if . . . ?" question in the previous section is just one way to do so. I have tried to take seriously the question and the way in which it is put by the one asking it.

But there are other ways to approach the hypothetical "what if . . . ?" situation. What follows are answers seven other people have given. They range from older writings by Tolstoy and Furness to more modern arguments by Baez and Auckerman. With seriousness or with humor, all of them attempt to deal head on with the classic question so often addressed to pacifists.

Certain Things Christians Cannot Do

by Count Leo Tolstoy

There are actions which are morally impossible, just as others are physically impossible. As a man cannot lift a mountain, and as a kindly man cannot kill an infant, so a man living the Christian life cannot take part in deeds of violence. Of what value then to him are arguments about the imaginary advantages of doing what is morally impossible for him to do?

But how is a man to act when he sees clearly an evil in following the law of love and its corollary law of nonresistance? How (to use the stock example) is a man to act when he sees a criminal killing or outraging a child and he can only save the child by killing the criminal?

When such a case is put, it is generally assumed that the only possible reply is that one should kill the assailant to save the child. But this answer is given so quickly and decidedly only because we are all so accustomed to the use of violence—not only to save a child, but even to prevent a neighboring government altering its frontier at the expense of ours, or to prevent someone from smuggling lace across that frontier, or even to defend our garden fruit from a passer-by. It is assumed that to save the child the assailant should be killed.

But it is only necessary to consider the question, "On what grounds ought a man, whether he be or be not a Christian, to act so?" in order to come to the conclusion that such action has no reasonable foundation. It only seems to us necessary because up to two thousand years ago such conduct was considered right, and a habit of acting so had been formed.

Why should a non-Christian, not acknowledging God, and not regarding the fulfillment of his will as the aim of life, decide to kill the criminal in order to defend the child? By killing the former he kills for certain; whereas he cannot know positively whether the criminal would have killed the child or not. But letting that pass, who shall say whether the child's life was more needed, was better, than the other's life? Surely, if the non-Christian knows not God and does not see life's meaning to be in the performance of his will, the only rule for his actions must be a reckoning, a conception, of which is more profitable for him and for all men, a continuation of the criminal's life or of the child's. To decide that, he needs to know what would become of the child whom he saves, and what, had he not killed him, would have been the future of the assailant. And as he cannot know this, the non-Christian has no sufficient rational ground for killing a robber to save a child.

If a man be a Christian and consequently acknowledges God and sees the meaning of life in fulfilling his will, then however ferocious the assailant, however innocent and lovely the child, he has even less ground to abandon the God-given law and to do to the criminal as the criminal wishes to do to the child. He may plead with the assailant, may interpose his own body between the assailant and the victim; but there is one thing he cannot do—he cannot deliberately abandon the law he has received from God, the fulfillment of which alone gives meaning to his life.

Very probably bad education, or his animal nature, may cause a man, Christian or non-Christian, to kill an assailant, not to save a child, but even to save himself or to save his purse. But it does not follow that he is right in acting thus or that he should accustom himself or others to think such conduct right. What it does show is that, notwithstanding a coating of education and of Christianity, the habits of the stone age are yet so strong in man that he still commits actions long since condemned by his reasonable conscience.

I see a criminal killing a child, and I can save the child by killing the assailant—therefore, in certain cases, violence must be used to resist evil. A man's life is in danger and can be saved only by my telling a lie—therefore, in certain cases, one must lie. A man is starving, and I can only save him by stealing—therefore, in certain cases, one must steal.

I lately read a story by Coppee in which an orderly kills his officer, whose life was insured, and thereby saves the honor and the family of the officer, the moral being that, in certain cases, one must kill. Such devices, and the deductions from them, only prove that there are men who know that it is not well to steal, to lie, or to kill but who are still so unwilling that people should cease to do these things that they use all their mental powers to invent excuses for such conduct. There is no moral law concerning which one might not devise a case in which it is difficult to decide which is more moral, to disobey the law or to obey it? But all such devices fail to prove that the laws, "Thou shalt not lie, steal, or kill," are invalid.

It is thus with the law of nonresistance. People know it is wrong to use violence, but they are so anxious to continue to live a life secured by "the strong arm of the law" that, instead of devoting their intellects to the elucidation of the evils which have flowed and are still flowing from admitting that man has a right to use violence to his fellow men, they prefer to exert their mental powers in defense of that error. *"Fais ce que dois, advienne que pourra"*—"Do what's right, come what may"—is an expression of profound wisdom. We each can know indubitably what we ought to do, but what results will follow from our actions we none of us either do or can know. Therefore it follows that, besides feeling the call of duty, we are further driven to act as duty bids us by the consideration that we have no other guidance but are totally ignorant of what will result from our action.

Christian teaching indicates what a man should do to perform the will of him who sent him into life; and discussion as to what results we anticipate from such or such human actions have nothing to do with Christianity but are just an example of the error which Christianity eliminates. None of us has ever yet met the imaginary criminal with the imaginary child, but all the horrors which fill the annals of history and of our own times came, and come, from this one thing: namely, that people will believe they really foresee speculative future results of actions.

The case is this. People once lived an animal life and violated or killed whom they thought well to violate or to kill. They even ate one another, and public opinion approved of it. Thousands of years ago, as far back as the times of Moses, a day came when people had realized that to violate or kill one another is bad. But there were people for whom the reign of force was advantageous, and these did not approve of the change but assured themselves and others that to do deeds of violence and to kill people is not always bad but that there are circumstances when it is necessary and even moral. And violence and slaughter, though not so frequent or so cruel as before, continued, only with this difference, that those who committed or commended such acts excused themselves by pleading that they did it for the benefit of humanity.

It was just this sophistical justification of violence that Christ denounced. When two enemies fight, each may think his own conduct justified by the circumstances. Excuses can be made for every use of violence, and no infallible standard has ever been discovered by which to measure the worth of these excuses. Therefore Christ taught us to disbelieve in any excuse for violence and (contrary to what had been taught by them of old times) never to use violence.

One would have thought that those who have professed Christianity would be indefatigable in exposing deception in this matter; for in such exposure lay one of the chief manifestations of Christianity. What really happened was just the reverse. People who profited by violence and who did not wish to give up their advantages took on themselves a monopoly of Christian preaching and declared that, as cases can be found in which nonresistance causes more harm than the use of violence (the imaginary criminal killing the imaginary child), therefore Christ's doctrine of nonresistance need not always be followed; and that one may deviate from his teaching to defend one's life or the life of others; or to defend one's country, to save society from lunatics or criminals, and in many other cases.

Leo Tolstoy (1828-1910), Russia's leading author of short stories and novels, came by his own intellectual and religious pilgrimage to strong nonresistant convictions, which he argued at great length in commentaries, systematic expositions, and occasional writings. This extract was part of a letter to the American international lawyer, Ernest Howard Crosby. It is taken from the book, *Tolstoy on Civil Disobedience and Nonviolence* (New York: Bergman/Signet/New American Library, 1967).

by S.H. Booth-Clibborn
Is It Too Late?

No! It's not yet too late for us Christians to consider our relation to the war question.*

Yes! It is too late for the pacifists: for their weapons, being merely political, have failed, as everything human is bound to fail.

Yes! and the socialists have failed too, having repeatedly scorned and rejected true Christian standards for those of a stupid and godless materialism. True, we have admired their devotion and zeal for peace. For the last two tragic years their burning enthusiasm (in America at least) has put us poor sleepy (though "professed") followers of the Prince of Peace to shame! But they are now bidden to "forever hold their peace," and that's the only brand of "peace" they are allowed to hold on to: for whatever is not built on "Christ the solid rock" is left to the fate of "sinking sand."

But what about us? Yes, us Christians, who have been preaching this gospel of LOVE, JOY, and PEACE so loud and so long? Now that it has come to practicing what we preach, now that the fiery test will be applied, are we willing

_____
*This article was published during World War I.

to go through with Jesus? Are we ready to "go forth therefore unto him without the camp, bearing his reproach"? (Heb. 13:13).

Should a Christian fight?

Let us examine carefully and prayerfully the principles of our holy faith, which principles we but yesterday rattled off so glibly, but which now means so much!

The subject is so vast and the space allowed so small that I shall confine myself to answering some of the popular objections to Christian nonresistance. However, be it clearly understood that the matter is treated from Christian standpoint only, and addressed only to Christians, the arguments being based solely on the authority of God's Holy Word!

Question: If war is wrong for the Christian, why did God himself in the Old Testament lead Israel into battle and into victory against their enemies?

Answer: The Jews were then living in the age of law and judgment: while we dwell in the dispensation of grace and mercy! Right here is where there is an appalling amount of thick ignorance among God's own people, resulting in this everlasting muddling up of Old Testament and New Testament teaching of law and grace, of judgment and mercy, of war and peace, all through failing to "rightly divide the word of truth." We find recorded in the 17th verse of the first chapter of John's Gospel that "the law was given by Moses, but grace and truth came by Jesus Christ." God ordered Israel to wipe out in direct judgment the morally rotten Canaanites: but find me in the New Testament where Christ ever sent his followers on such a mission? On the contrary he sent them out to save men—not to butcher them like cattle. Again Jehovah openly declared himself on Israel's side, by startling miracles, both at Jericho and with Gideon, as well as at many other times and places. What nation now in the bloody mess can produce such proofs of its being in the right, or of God being on its side?

No! as far as the Christian is concerned, the "eye for an eye" system has given place to the "turn to him the other cheek also" of Matthew 5:39-44. The reader is urged here to compare the following passages in order to realize the wide difference existing between Israel and the church of Christ:

ISRAEL   **CHURCH**

Difference in Calling
Genesis 12:1   Philippians 3:20

Difference in Conduct
Deuteronomy 7:1, 2   Matthew 5:38-44

Difference in Worship
Leviticus 17:8, 9   Matthew 18:20

Question. Oh, it's all very well in theory, but suppose a brute in human form attacked your wife and children. Would you stand by and allow it? Having fired this broadside the patriot awaits the answer with an air of triumphant finality, while I'm supposed to rush blindly into the favorite trap. But praise God, he who is in the habit of receiving "tips" from heaven soon gets wise to such tricks; and now is for the . . .*

Answer: In the first place the illustration does not fit the case at all, for the murderous individual tries to assault my

*At this point something is missing in the original text.

family of his own free will, whereas in this war poor harmless people are driven like cattle and quite against their will by godless governments into butchering each other. A more fitting picture of the situation would be found in a Spanish-American cock fight, where the poor benighted birds scatter each other's blood and feathers at their owners' pleasure—these latter together with the "neutral" spectators reaping all the profits.

In the second place, to substitute facts for wild supposition, thousands of humble Christian homes have never yet been broken into by a criminal of any sort: God protecting his own according to their faith; for they put their trust in him rather than in the police.

Third, if it should come to actual violence—Matthew 5 and Romans 12 would still remain true, and God's Word would still have to be obeyed (cf. the case of the three Hebrew children, Dan. 3:16-23.)

Of course I have not included the many religious persecutions which down the ages have been the inevitable accompaniment of every new and powerful movement: and yet these very persecutions have set the seal of God's approval in the most striking way on the doctrine of Christian nonresistance. Those early nonresisters, mind you, were the same martyrs, of whom, in these days of inherited religion, the boast is so often heard that "their blood was the seed of the church." Their sublime endurance under the most exquisite sufferings should ... silence forever our contemptible excuses for crawling cowardice.

"And he said to me, These are they which come out of great tribulation ... therefore are they before the throne of God ... They shall hunger no more, neither thirst any more.... For the lamb which is in the midst of the throne shall feed them, and shall lead them unto living fountains of

waters: and God shall wipe away all tears from their eyes"
(Rev. 7:14-17).

This article appeared in the *Weekly Evangel*, April 28, 1917, p. 5. Booth-
Clibborn was a leader in the early British Pentecostal movement,
grandson of the founder of the Salvation Army.

by C. J. Furness

Faith in the Power of the Spirit

Militarist: Well now, just imagine that Hitler should come to invade America with his armies. That is possible. He is approaching our shores. What do you propose to do? Are you just going to pray and let him land and do whatever he wants to with us?

Pacifist: No, that is just the point. I want you to understand that I am not a negative "passivist." I do not believe that we should just "stand and take it," much less "lie down and take it"!

I believe it is possible to overcome evil with good. But it is necessary to have faith in it. I know that spiritual power is a *positive* force. I have depended on it in everything I do. Christ said that if you had enough faith you could say to a mountain, "Remove," and it would be removed. I do not claim to have enough faith to move mountains, but I do believe that Christ meant what he said and that he knew what he was talking about. Many people claim to be Christians but don't really believe that Christ's teachings are practical. They don't have enough faith in them to try to apply them.

You have asked me whether I think we ought to submit passively to Hitler and obey his orders. I certainly believe that we should refuse to obey his orders or anybody else's insofar as they conflict with our consciences. We should have to be prepared to pay the supreme price, if necessary, for our faith. I do not claim that we might not be attacked and killed, but I should consider that to be a much lesser evil than killing the invaders myself. Inevitably there must come times when the consequences of physical nonresistance are death. One of my Quaker ancestors was killed during the Revolution by a recruiting officer because he refused to bear arms.

Neither do I mean that I would just stand on the shore and pray that Hitler would turn around and go back. I would prepare myself to meet him with a full realization of "that-of-God" which is in him, as it is in every man. Only in this spirit would the way be made possible to meet him on common spiritual ground. If he did not then respond, I must be prepared to lose my own life rather than to allow him to force me to do what my conscience forbids.

Militarist: Now I would like to ask you a question. If your mother were sick in bed and couldn't move and a gangster were approaching her to attack her, would you still say it was your duty not to kill him? We will say, of course, that you have exhausted all reasonable possibilities of dissuading him and that he has refused to respond. If you have a weapon in your hand, is it not then your duty to take his life in order to save your mother?

Pacifist: I have often talked this over with my mother and she agrees with me that I should let the gangster kill her rather than to have his blood on my hands. That is a comparatively easy situation to solve. I know all the stock situations that are brought up in this connection and the arguments about them, so I would like to clear this up by a more challenging test case. The hypothesis about my mother is comparatively simple and has never given me much difficulty to solve, but I can think of other situations which have been a source of a good deal of argument with myself.

It is difficult for me to settle with my own conscience what I really ought to do if, for instance, the object of attack is a very young child; let us suppose also that the attacker is not a gangster but a maniac. It is a very great temptation to use force even to the extent of murdering the maniac in order to protect the child who is young, helpless, and innocent. I do not know just why there should be such a pronounced difference as exists in my mind between this case and that of my mother and the gangster, but I do know that somehow it is much harder to say that my duty is to spare the life of the insane person if it means sacrificing the life of the child.

Militarist: Perhaps the difference is that your mother has already reached the age to decide for herself; she has definitely approved your conscientious stand. She has expressed her willingness to give up her life for your principle. But the child has not reached any age where he could decide such a difficult point for himself. Don't you think that may have something to do with it?

Pacifist: Perhaps. I really can't explain the difference in words because I do not thoroughly understand myself the legal points or moral principles involved. Perhaps your explanation is the right one; but I must say also, in order to make clear to you how I believe that I should conduct myself in such a situation, that I do not regard "crazy" people in the same light as most people do. I have associated a good deal with mental cases, and I have for a long time been particularly interested in the problem of how to handle the insane. Dr. Clara Barrus, who was an eminent authority and alienist, was a friend of mine. She wrote the first book of real scientific competence on *Nursing the Insane*. In her long career as doctor at the hospital for the insane in Middletown, New York, she never used violence of any kind with the patients or permitted force to be used by others for her protection.

Also I knew a nurse whose father and husband both became insane. She told me how she kept her husband at home because she felt faith in her ability to handle him, and she knew that he would be treated with physical violence if committed to an institution. I shall never forget how she described hearing him come into the bathroom behind her one day. She looked around and saw that he held a long butcher knife in his hand. He said, "Mary, we've always been wonderful pals. I'm going to put an end to it all now so that it will be perfect!" She told me that she prayed as she had never prayed in her life and immediately put the power of faith into action. "Put down that knife," she said to him, knowing that her love could touch his spirit behind the mask of insanity. He let her take the knife away from him. I believe that the spirit is never ill or insane and that the power of faith and spiritual appeal can reach through to the most hardened cases.

Militarist: Does this unusual belief about insanity come from your Quaker training also?

Pacifist: Perhaps that has something to do with it, for Friends have believed from the earliest days of the Society that there is "that-of-God in *every* man." George Fox tells in his *Journal* how "there was a distracted woman under a doctor's hand with her hair loose all about her ears; and he was about to let her blood, she being first bound, and many people being about her, holding her by violence. But he could get no blood from her. And I desired them to unbind her and let her alone, for they could not touch the spirit in her, by which she was tormented. So they did unbind her. And I was moved to speak to her, and in the name of the

Lord to bid her be quiet and still. And she was so. And the Lord's power settled her mind, and she mended."

Militarist: Do I understand then that you would take the risk of letting this child in your hypothetical test case be killed rather than to kill the maniac?

Pacifist: I do not have the brashness to claim that I would not kill the insane person to save the child, if I had it in my power to do so—but I believe that I ought not to kill him, and I should pray for power to stick to that course of action. I do not believe that I should have any right to take this stand, however, unless I *do* have faith in the efficacy of spiritual power that can be invoked in time of need. Neither do I have any right to make this decision unless I am willing to take the responsibility and accept the fatal results if such an appeal to spiritual power should fail. My answer then is, unequivocally, that I should not kill the maniac.

Militarist: You have at least one virtue: you are consistent.

Pacifist: I do not claim to be absolutely consistent, for that is practically impossible for any human being. But I have given serious thought to this problem for years. I went through it when I was eighteen years old, and I did not have much experience along these lines to offer as evidence. Therefore I know how tough it is to try to prove such things. I know that you think my faith in a power to overcome evil with good is an illusion. You consider my philosophy of life impractical. But I have lived by it as consistently as I could for thirty years, and I know that it works!

Clifton Joseph Furness, of the New England Conservatory of Music, recorded in 1942 the "Inquisition" from which this exchange is extracted. It was published in 1944 in *The Gist: A Peace Digest* by the Fellowship of Reconciliation and the National Council for the Prevention of War. Reprinted by permission of the Fellowship of Reconciliation.

by
Henry
T.
Hodgkin

No Revolver as a Last Resort

The only sure guidance in difficult situations is the deeper knowledge of persons which may come through spiritual illumination. If all life should be and may be related to our Father's will, we can count upon this illumination, and it may frequently be given in ways that will surprise us and make it possible to eliminate the use of force even where it had seemed the only possible way to handle the situation.

I almost hesitate to give the following incident, because it seems as if it had been invented to illustrate the point. I heard the story a few years ago and can vouch for its accuracy. A certain man had recently been converted in a Salvation Army meeting. Going home one night, he found his father intoxicated and actually attacking his mother with a hatchet. He went up to his father and said to him quietly, "You know you oughtn't to do that, dad." His father put down the weapon, sobered by his son's words and spirit, and the incident led to a change in the man's own life.

Here is a case where the use of force would seem, on general principles, to be justifiable and indeed the only means of dealing with a desperate situation. A man who has recently come into a new and vital experience of God in his own soul enters the room. Responding, as I hold, to that inner guidance which transcends all formula, he deals with the situation in what we should be tempted to call an absurd way. And, be it noted, he not only defends the defenseless woman, but he avoids the danger of still further infuriating a drunken man and perhaps doing him serious harm. He also is the means of permanently solving the problem. His act creates a good husband out of the violent drunkard.

How many of our so-called insoluble problems could be handled in a similar way, I have no means of knowing; but it is clear that, given a real interest in the offender and a passionate desire to change his evil mind into a right one, there are many situations that could be dealt with quietly which seem, on the face of it, to demand what we should call more vigorous methods. The fact is that the resort to force in most cases implies a disbelief in God and in man. It is a surrender of the higher method for a lower, easier, and, be it noted, a less ultimately effective way of meeting evil.

I remember discussing a similar problem with a friend during the recent war, and he said to me, "Yes, I should wish to use all the spiritual force which I could command, but I should like to have a revolver in my pocket to use if the worst came to the worst."

Now the view of the place of coercion that I am here maintaining is emphatically not that of my friend. It is not a case of turning to coercion as a last resort but using it, if at all, as part of the method of love. The "last resort" in the mind of Jesus seems to have been the supreme appeal of forgiving love. If that failed, nothing else would succeed for the end he had in view. With a revolver in our pocket, so to speak, we miss the power to make the final appeal of good will.

Henry T. Hodgkin was one of the founders of the International Fellowship of Reconciliation. The excerpt reproduced here is from his book *The Christian Revolution* (London: Swarthmore Press, 1923).

by Joan Baez | Three Cheers for Grandma!

"Okay, you're a pacifist. What would you do if someone were, say, attacking your grandmother?"

"Attacking my poor old grandmother?"

"Yeah. You're in a room with your grandmother, and there's this guy about to attack her, and you're standing there. What would you do?"

"I'd yell, 'Three cheers for Grandma!' and leave the room."

"No, seriously. Say he had a gun, and he was about to shoot her. Would you shoot him first?"

"Do I have a gun?"

"Yes."

"No. I'm a pacifist, I don't have a gun."

"Well, say you do."

"All right. Am I a good shot?"

"Yes."

"I'd shoot the gun out of his hand."

"No, then you're not a good shot."

"I'd be afraid to shoot. Might kill grandma."

"Come on. Okay, look. We'll take another example. Say you're driving a truck. You're on a narrow road with a sheer

62

cliff on your side. There's a little girl standing in the middle of the road. You're going too fast to stop. What would you do?"

"I don't know. What would *you* do?"

"I'm asking you. You're the pacifist."

"Yes, I know. All right. Am I in control of the truck?"

"Yes."

"How about if I honk my horn so she can get out of the way?"

"She's too young to walk. And the horn doesn't work."

"I swerve around to the left of her, since she's not going anywhere."

"No, there's been a landslide."

"Oh. Well, then, I would try to drive the truck over the cliff and save the little girl."

Silence.

"Well, say there's someone else in the truck with you. Then what?"

"What's my decision have to do with my being a pacifist?"

"There's two of you in the truck and only one little girl."

"Someone once said, 'If you have a choice between a real evil and a hypothetical evil, always take the hypothetical one.' "

"Huh?"

"I said why are you so anxious to kill off all the pacifists?"

"I'm not. I just want to know what you'd do."

"If I were with a friend in a truck driving very fast on a one-lane road approaching a dangerous impasse where a ten-month-old girl is sitting in the middle of the road with a landslide one side of her and a sheer drop-off on the other."

"That's right."

"I would probably slam on the brakes, thus sending my

friend through the front windshield, skid into the landslide, run over the little girl, sail off the cliff, and plunge to my own death. No doubt grandma's house would be at the bottom of the ravine, and the truck would crash through her roof and blow up in her living room, where she was finally being attacked for the first, and last, time."

"You haven't answered my question. You're just trying to get out of it."

"I'm really trying to say a couple of things. One is that no one knows what he'll do in a moment of crisis. And that hypothetical questions get hypothetical answers. I'm also hinting that you have made it impossible for me to come out of the situation without having killed one or more people. Then you say, 'Pacifism is a nice idea, but it won't work.' But that's not what bothers me."

"What bothers you?"

"Well, you may not like it because it's not hypothetical. It's real. And it makes the assault on grandma look like a garden party."

"What's that?"

"I'm thinking about how we put people through a training process so they'll find out the really good, efficient ways of killing. Nothing incidental like trucks and landslides—just the opposite, really. You know, how to growl and yell, kill and crawl and jump out of airplanes—real organized stuff. Why, you have to be able to run a bayonet through grandma's middle."

"That's something entirely different."

"Sure. And don't you see that it's so much harder to look at, because it's real, and it's going on right now? Look. A general sticks a pin into a map. A week later a bunch of young boys are sweating it out in a jungle somewhere, shooting each other's arms and legs off, crying and praying and losing control of their bowels. Doesn't it seem stupid to you?"

"Well, you're talking about war."

"Yes, I know. Doesn't it seem stupid?"

"What do you do instead, then? Turn the other cheek, I suppose."

"No. Love thine enemy but confront his evil. Love thine enemy. Thou shalt not kill."

"Yeah, and look what happened to him."

"He grew up."

"They hung him on a damn cross is what happened to him. I don't want to get hung on a damn cross."

"You won't."

"Huh?"

"I said you don't get to choose how you're going to die. Or when. You can only decide how you're going to live. Now."

"Well, I'm not going to go letting everybody step all over me, that's for sure."

"Jesus said, 'Resist not evil.' The pacifist says just the opposite. He says to resist evil with all your heart and with all your mind and body until it has been overcome."

"I don't get it."

"Organized nonviolent resistance. Gandhi. He organized the Indians for nonviolent resistance and waged nonviolent war against the British until he'd freed India from the British Empire. Not bad for a first try, don't you think?"

"Yeah, fine, but he was dealing with the British, a civilized people. We're not."

"Not a civilized people?"

"Not dealing with a civilized people. You just try some of that stuff on the Russians."

"You mean the Chinese, don't you?"

"Yeah, the Chinese. Try it on the Chinese."

"Oh, dear. War was going on long before anybody dreamed up communism. It's just the latest justification for self-righteousness. The problem isn't communism. The problem is consensus. There's a consensus out that it's okay to kill when your government decides who to kill. If you kill inside the country, you get in trouble. If you kill outside the country, right time, right season, latest enemy, you get a medal. There are about one hundred and thirty nation-states, and each of them thinks it's a swell idea to bump off all the rest because he is more important.

"The pacifist thinks there is only one tribe. Four billion members. They come first. We think killing any member of the family is a dumb idea. We think there are more decent and intelligent ways of settling differences. And man had better start investigating these other possibilities because if he doesn't, then by mistake or by design he will probably kill off the whole damn race."

"It's human nature to kill."

"Is it?"

"It's natural. Something you can't change."

"If it's natural to kill, why do men have to go into training to learn how? There's violence in human nature, but there's also decency, love, kindness. Man organizes, buys, sells, pushes violence. The nonviolenter wants to organize the opposite side. That's all nonviolence is—organized love."

"You're crazy."

"No doubt. Would you care to tell me the rest of the world is sane? Tell me that violence has been a great success for the past five thousand years; that the world is in fine shape, that wars have brought peace, understanding, brotherhood, democracy, and freedom to mankind; that killing each other has created an atmosphere of trust and hope.

That it's grand for one billion people to live off the other three billion, or that even if it hasn't been smooth going all along, we are now at last beginning to see our way through to a better world for all—as soon as we get a few minor wars out of the way."

"I'm doing okay."

"Consider it a lucky accident."

"I believe I should defend America and all that it stands for. Don't you believe in self-defense?"

"No, that's how the Mafia got started. A little band of people who got together to protect peasants. I'll take Gandhi's nonviolent resistance."

"I still don't get the point of nonviolence."

"The point of nonviolence is to build a floor, a strong new floor, beneath which we can no longer sink. A platform which stands a few feet above napalm, torture, exploitation, poison gas, A and H bombs, the works. Give man a decent place to stand. He's been wallowing around in human blood and vomit and burnt flesh, screaming how it's going to bring peace to the world. He sticks his head out of the hole for a minute and sees an odd bunch of people gathering material and attempting to build a structure above ground in the fresh air. 'Nice idea but not very practical,' he shouts and slides back into the hole.

"It was the same kind of thing when man found out the world was round. He fought for years to have it remain flat, with every proof on hand that it was not flat at all. It had no edge to drop off or sea monsters to swallow up his little ship in their gaping jaws."

"How are you going to build this practical structure?"

"From the ground up. By studying, learning about, experimenting with every possible alternative to violence on every level. By learning how to say no to the nation-state, no to war taxes, no to the draft, no to killing in general, yes to the brotherhood of man; by starting new institutions which are based on the assumption that murder in any form is ruled out; by making and keeping in touch with nonviolent contacts all over the world; by engaging ourselves at every possible chance in dialogue with people, groups, to try to begin to change the consensus that it's okay to kill."

"It sounds real nice, but I just don't think it can work."

"You are probably right. We probably don't have enough time. So far we've been a glorious flop. The only thing that's been a worse flop than the organization of nonviolence has been the organization of violence."

Folk singer Joan Baez has since the 1960s combined entertainment with advocacy. This text from her book *Daybreak*(© 1968) also appeared in *The Atlantic Monthly* in August 1968.

Why Not Add a Bit?

by Dale W. Brown

Hypothetical questions deserve hypothetical answers. For hypothetical questions are set up in such a way as to manipulate the outcome. Hypothetical alternatives may be needed to demonstrate that the game can work both ways.

For example, you arrive suddenly on a terrible scene. A group of children are playing. A man is pointing a gun in their direction. If you shoot him, you will save the children. If you fail, you may be responsible for their death. You shoot. The man is dead.

As long as it is hypothetical, however, why not add a bit more? There was a ferocious bear coming up the hill which the man could see and you could not. He was actually going to shoot the bear in order to save the children. Since your shot killed him, however, the bear mauled several children to their death. Tragically, you only had one shot.

Though it could be fun to continue this kind of gamesmanship, it might be helpful to consider slightly more seriously some of the additional hypothetical questions posed to pacifists. This one is common: "What would happen if everyone laid down his arms?"

One's first response is to exclaim, "Wonderful! This means that at last there would be peace in the world." It is protested that the question has been phrased wrongly. "What if all Americans became pacifists? Would not the

69

Russians, Chinese, or others walk in and take us over?"
From my personal acquaintance with Americans, it is very
difficult to imagine all Americans ever becoming pacifists,
but I have to treat the question as if such were a possible im-
possibility.

It might be that such an example of the most powerful nation in the world believing in the way of suffering love
would have such an impact that the conquering armies
could not be disciplined sufficiently to do their job, and
world opinion would be aroused to stop the action. Or it
might mean the most massive slaughter, martyrdom, and
noblest witness to Christianity this world has ever seen. Or
again it might mean that Americans for the first time would
have to live under the type of dictatorship which their
money has helped to keep in power in Spain, South
Vietnam, Guatemala, and many other places in the world.

Frankly, I don't know what would happen if all of
America became Christlike in taking up the cross of suffering love. But I do know that the feelings of the questioner
and the pacifist are based upon two entirely different
assumptions. The questioner usually looks upon the possibility of every American's following in the steps of Jesus as
the greatest tragedy possible. I view the possibility of
America's becoming this Christian as wonderful. I can't
begin to predict what might take place. But I would like to
see it happen.

But what about Hitler? With the genocide of 6,000,000
Jews and the ruthless imposition of his dictatorship on many
other countries, how could one fail to resist this type of evil?

Such questions cannot be answered flippantly. We do not
have here an entirely hypothetical case: Hitler actually
existed, and we know something of the horrors of the period.
The question is most selective, however, in that it isolates

one situation in history in order to make a case.

A pacifist may be tempted to counter with a different case likewise anchored in history. For example, if America had been pacifist and had kept out of World War I, the world might never have known the unjust peace treaty and severe reparations which helped to create the conditions for a Hitler to come to power. Another bit of speculation will indicate the way to plead a position by the type of "if" question selected. If America had not entered World War II, Germany and Russia might have destroyed each other to the extent that Communism would have been crushed and Germany so weakened as to ease her stranglehold on Europe.

Such reasoning, however, begs the original question. Most pacifists would advocate a loving resistance to Hitler, noble examples of which were in evidence in the underground movements of conquered Scandinavian countries. One dare not assume that such nonviolent resistance would have reduced the tyranny or even the suffering of the period. A Christian pacifist cannot promise that the way of the cross will be effective in any given situation. He cannot assume that his position will be widely accepted. He does live in the faith that the way of the cross is the right response and that, if tried, it ultimately would be best for all.

There is an attitude of patience involved here. Politically, one would live in the faith that evil regimes do have within themselves the seeds of their own destruction. There is evidence, for example, of several plots to overthrow Hitler's tyranny by his own officials. But one cannot depend on such political analyses. For we can never know the answer to the "what if" questions of the past or the future. We can trust in his way in hope that this is *the* way.

The same problem is raised today in a new form by

persons who advocate violent revolution for dispossessed people under repressive regimes. It is argued that a lesser violence comes through violent revolution than is possible by allowing present injustices to continue. Institutionalized violence to persons, it is asserted, can be more vicious than overt physical violence. For the former is that violence against persons which is perpetuated by the power structure in the form of psychological slavery, high infant mortality rates, poor medical care, ghetto-type living, and low life expectancy.

China, which suffered through a ruthless violent revolution, is cited by some to be better off than India, where basic revolutionary changes have not come about and where exist widespread poverty, lack of land reform, and institutionalized violence. Such arguments by revolutionaries today are difficult to answer. The pacifist, however, lives in the faith that, in the long run, just means are more likely to gain just ends.

In raising hypothetical questions, many persons assume direct application from one's personal action to one's stance on the question of war. If one believes in defending his wife, it is assumed that he should believe in a defensive war. Even if a pacifist would defend his wife, this does not mean that he would immediately move to bomb her attacker's wife and relatives.

More important, moreover, is the point that such reasoning overlooks the fact that some pacifists advocate police action for the state but still oppose all wars. They make a distinction between coercive action against the guilty individual from whom society needs to be protected and the wholesale killing of the innocent with the guilty, which is involved in modern warfare.

It should be recognized that there are different kinds of

pacifist responses. Some advocate a style of nonresistance. Some would attempt to deal with the attacker in a calm spirit of reason and prayer. Others would defend their families physically to the point of eliminating the attacker if necessary. Some of these would do everything short of actually killing the adversary. Some pacifists would participate in police action but not in war. Others could not participate in police action themselves but would grant its legitimacy for the state in an evil world.

Thus a pacifist stance against participation in war is held by a wide variety of people whose beliefs about their personal responses to force vary. For myself I would hope ideally to be faithful to a more absolute position against ever taking the life of another. I cannot assert dogmatically what I would do in any given situation. I would hope that God's grace would cause me to place obedience to the way of the life-giving cross above my own self-preservation.

An additional danger of hypothetical questions is that they may be a way for us to escape dealing with the real questions. Instead of dreaming up or responding to hypothetical questions for topics to debate, we need to be discussing the real ones. Is it right to destroy villages in order to save them? Should millions of men be trained to hate and to kill?

In dealing with hypothetical *and* real questions, however, there is a danger that we may get so hung up in discussing them that we forget to ask the really real question for the Christian: "What does it mean to be a disciple of Christ in our kind of world?"

Foremost, we need to keep in mind that there is no pat way to deal with hypothetical or real questions asked of pacifists. It is obvious that some of the answers, as well as the questions, are contrived and superficial. An invaluable ingredient for such discussions is a sense of humor. Sensitive to the total lives of our adversaries and open to new insights we may gain, we need to learn how to share in love what truth we may have. But witness we must—be it a silent presence or a prophecy of woe.

Though we have pointed to the pitfalls of playing the hypothetical game, we now yield to the temptation. In raising the hypothetical "if," the pacifist might talk like this: "What if a man would come and choose among others for his disciples a member of the Students for a Democratic Society, a militant Black Power advocate, and an official in the Internal Revenue Service? What if he would teach them that the way to overcome evil is with good? What if this same one would say he was going to set at liberty those who are oppressed? What if he would advocate in his own home church the dividing up of all the farm land and property anew? What if this man would go into the churches of the land and turn over the offering plates which are filled with the profits from the military-industrial complex? What if?"

There are more than one set of hypothetical questions.

_____

Dale W. Brown is professor of theology at Bethany Theological Seminary, Oak Brook, Illinois. This excerpt is part of a longer discussion of appealing to hard cases to debate the ethics of violence. It is taken from his book *Brethren and Pacifism,* copyrighted by The Brethren Press, Elgin, Ill. Used by permission.

The Scandal of Defense-lessness

by Dale Aukerman

Jesus acted decisively to defend any under attack, but not by crushing the attackers. There is in the Gospels an incident somewhat comparable to the situation asked about in the ever-repeated question, "What would you do if somebody attacked your wife, mother, sister...?"

Jesus was on the scene when the life of a defenseless woman was about to be taken (Jn. 8:2-11). Stones were in those tensed hands ready for hurling at the terrified adulteress. Jesus did not stand by and do nothing. But neither did he call down fire from heaven or rally his disciples to grab up whatever defensive stones they could find lying around. He halted the drive to crush the life out of her. He met their lethal force with a far different kind of power. There was no crushing of the attackers.

True, his was a limited triumph that day. His initiative did not draw those men into fellowship, but it did hold them back from total negation of fellowship. Jesus stood between the woman and the attackers. In effect he took the brunt of their attack upon himself. The bitter madness which extinguished his life was in part the very madness which he had held back from that woman.

Similarly, Jesus in Gethsemane defended the disciples by drawing the attack to himself: "If you seek me, let these men go" (Jn. 18:8). He defended them by absorbing the evil that was pressing toward them all.

When defense is needed, Christians should look to Jesus as the model. In Jesus we are shown what it is to be the kind of person God wants. "He who says he abides in him ought to walk in the same way in which he walked" (1 Jn. 2:6). Would God ever expect from us a mode of defense which we do not at all see in Jesus?

The questions with regard to a hypothetical attack often focus on the prospect of the rape of a man's wife, mother, sister. But there could have come a rape attempt on the mother or a sister of Jesus with him nearby. Jesus would have met that enemy in love, *or* by his own standards he would have sinned.

The intent of the hypothetical questions is to show that there are situations in which it is necessary to resort to a lesser evil inflicted on the attacker. But if this is indeed the case, Jesus was without sin only because of his good fortune in not having had to face that type of situation; and he was therefore not tempted in every respect as we are (cf. Heb. 4:15).

The *skandalon* (stumbling block) for the church through most of its history has not been the defenselessness of Jesus (which has been regarded as necessary for the salvation drama) but rather the corollary that his people should be defenseless in the same way. The prevailing protests within the church against acceptance of that defenselessness have come as a sort of echo of Peter's outburst: "God forbid, Lord! This mustn't happen to *us*." Peter with his plea was for Jesus a *skandalon* (Mt. 16:23), a lure tempting him to turn from God. In wrongheadedness too he was a representative first-start for the church; and for followers of Jesus that modification of Peter's plea against suffering at the hands of adversaries has continued to be the primary lure away from God.

If we try to defend others with violence, we replay Peter's reliance on the sword, which was really the turning point in his abandonment of Jesus. If Peter had stayed with the threatened One without resort to violence, his action could have been a model for how Christians are to stand with any who are threatened. Christ stands weaponless with them. His disciples are to do the same.

Jesus Christ is head of the community, and Christians are bound together in a corporate vulnerability derivative from his. Only when this is discerned can there be right thinking about defense of those attacked. Others may join together in military "defense," but Christians must stand together in shared vulnerability. In that common stand there are elements of defense. But in Gethsemane the disciples pulled out of this corporate vulnerability; they broke with the body rather than be broken themselves. And that has been the continuous pattern of Christendom/post-Christendom history down to the present.

Dale Aukerman has been active in Christian peace witness in the United States and Europe for most of three decades. He is currently involved in speaking and writing and in staff work with the Brethren Peace Fellowship. This excerpt from his book, *Darkening Valley*, copyright © 1981 by Dale Aukerman, is used by permission of The Seabury Press.

What Would You Do If?

by
Dale
Aukerman

In discussions two basic questions have been asked again and again as rebuttal to pacifism: "What would you do if someone attacked your wife and children?" and "What about the Russians? Would you just sit back and let them take over?"

The assumed answer is that any man in his right mind would be ready to fight and, if necessary, kill to fend off such an attack on loved ones, and that if we must be ready to do that for the family, we must be ready to do that against enemies of the country.

In seeking to give what I see as a Christian response to those questions, I admit first of all that I cannot say for sure in advance what I would or would not do in such hypothetical situations. However, as a disciple of Jesus, I can say beforehand what I think would be wrong, out of bounds, unchristian to do, and what I hope I would be able to do.

As a Christian, I know that in any family attack situation, it would be wrong for me to move against the life and person of that attacker. To do so would be utterly contrary to the teaching and way of Christ. And I surely would not try to kill the wife and children of the attacker—which would be the analogy for much that is done in war.

Exactly what the content of my response would be cannot and need not be worked out in advance. But my hope is that it would show something of the love of Christ to the attacker. How I think beforehand about what I would hope to do does not guarantee that I would come through with that in the real situations, but it does very much incline me toward such response.

The crucial question here is whether Jesus is seen as Lord. Jesus gave the command: "Love your enemies, do good to those who hate you, bless those who curse you, pray for those who abuse you" (Luke 6:27-28, NRSV). He lived that teaching in the way he faced his enemies.

That ever-repeated question does have great emotional power: What would I do if someone was about to rape and kill my wife, or kill a child of mine? However, if I am a Christian, there is a prior and more determinative question: Do I see Jesus as Lord of my life also for such a situation? If I hold to this Lord, I cannot move against the life of the attacker.

Christ helping me, I am to love, bless, pray for, and do good to the attacker. To find, in such moments, creative ways to do this is the opposite of being passive. Maybe I wouldn't come through; perhaps I would be immobilized by fear. But disciples have the promise of Jesus given in Scripture and repeated to Pascal: "I shall act in thee if it occur."

Perhaps a Christian says, "If my wife or child were about to be killed, I'd certainly try to kill the guy to prevent that." The person is really saying, "I couldn't have Jesus as Lord of my life in that situation; I couldn't allow myself to be limited in such a way." That would-be disciple is deciding beforehand to go opposite from the way of Christ and, in that manner of thinking, has already turned from Christ. If we look to Jesus as Lord, we cannot have guns in our homes with the idea of using them to protect ourselves and our loved ones.

If husband, wife, and other members of the family are together committed to Christ's way of peace, they share the vulnerability which goes with that. The husband doesn't need to be ready to use a gun for the wife to see him as a real man. I recall the comment of a young Brethren woman in Indiana who said, "I would not want my father or a brother to kill someone in order to defend me."

The church in local fellowships should be committed to this way of Jesus. Then members can stand together supporting each other in a stance that is so much in contrast to the violence of the world.

If someone dear to me is attacked, I shouldn't passively acquiesce. I should act—but act in love. In some circumstances that might mean putting myself between the attacker and the intended victim. It could mean trying physically to restrain or even to disarm the attacker.

I've talked with men who as conscientious objectors during World War II did their alternative service in mental hospitals (Civilian Public Service, CPS). They took with them their commitment to nonviolence. But when a severely disturbed patient grabbed a knife, they would use a mattress, pin the patient against a wall, and get the knife. Such physical restraining can be done in love and with clear expression of love.

Killing or trying to kill an attacker cannot be done in love or with clear expression of love. Women committed to Christian nonviolence may do well to take a course in women's self-defense, though they may reject for themselves some of the options presented.

In the realm of hypothesis, someone could have been about to rape the mother or a sister of Jesus with him nearby. Would Jesus have tried, if it seemed necessary, to kill the attacker? Surely not. If he had done such a thing, the "One without sin" would have sinned.

What we find in the Gospels is that Jesus acted decisively to defend anyone under attack, but not by crushing the attackers. Jesus was on the scene when the life of a defenseless woman was about to be taken. Stones were in those tensed hands ready for hurling at the terrified adulteress (John 8:1-11).

Jesus did not stand by and do nothing. But neither did he call down fire from heaven or rally his disciples to grab up what stones they could find lying around. He halted the Pharisees' drive to crush the life out of the woman. He met their lethal force with a far different kind of power. The Lord calls us and enables us to meet violence with the same kind of power.

The question about the family being attacked typically assumes that if a man is enough of a man and is ready to use a weapon, he can save those under attack. But that is a typical Hollywood picture of the good guy outshooting the bad guy. In real life, however, the attacker would ordinarily have the upper hand, and an impulsive resort to violence would be most problematical.

One study showed that when a gun is used for home defense, those being defended are more likely to be killed than when a gun is not used. The person who uses a gun to stop an attacker may succeed, but in many cases does not succeed. The person who tries to stop a violent attack by initiatives of love may succeed, or quite often may fail. But the nonviolent defender, even in failure, stands with the Lord of the universe, whose climactic defeat by his adversaries was drawn up into the supreme victory of the resurrection.

We take a big risk if we resort to lethal defense. We also take a big risk if we reject such violence and seek to live the love of Christ. But rejecting the way of Christ constitutes the biggest risk of all.

I was told the story of a Czech couple asleep in a bedroom of their inn. The wife awakened and saw a man with a knife coming through the open window and toward them in the darkness. As he approached the bed, she called, "You can kill us, but first let me make you a cup of coffee." The man accepted the offer, and then gave up what he intended to do. The point is not so much that the wife's initiative worked as that it was profoundly right.

Nevertheless, another question was for decades usually paired with the one about loved ones being attacked: "What about the Russians?" What about whoever is the current national enemy and the terrible things they might do to us? Behind this question is the assumption that the nation keeps us safe from the horrors that the enemy could inflict on us, or more especially upon our loved ones, and that therefore we must do everything needed to defend and preserve our nation.

Christians dare not give to the nation that sort of supreme importance. To do so is idolatry. We are to look to God as the one who brings us through.

Still, however, the second of the paired questions confronts us with the issue of our concern for loved ones. If we are Christians, we cannot assume that the nation is the main guarantor of our security and has to be preserved. But we do love those closest to us (and others too), and we don't want them to be overrun by a hostile people.

Disciples in a personal attack situation must not move against the life and person of the attacker. However, in all the freedom of imaginative love, they can seek to defend. In the matter of defending the country, disciples dare not align themselves with the national recourse to lethal violence, totally contrary to God's revelation in Jesus.

Yet disciples are ready to join in nonviolent resistance, civilian-based defense against invasion and occupation by another country. In World War II, European Christians were very active in nonviolent resistance to the Nazis, and many lost their lives doing that.

Festo Kivengere, Anglican bishop of Uganda, knew firsthand the terrors of Idi Amin's regime. In exile he was asked: "If you were sitting in Idi Amin's office with a gun in your hand, what would you do?" He replied: "I would give the gun to Amin and say, 'This is your weapon; my weapon is love.' "

Before the United States entered World War II, George Kennan as a diplomat visited all the capitals in Nazi-occupied Europe. He has written that he was convinced at the time that, whatever the outcome of the war, the Nazis would not be able to maintain control over these countries. That was too big a task. And he added that the Soviets, if they would overrun Western Europe, would not be able to keep the populations down; they were barely able to keep control of Eastern Europe.

As we have seen, in 1989 the Soviets lost control of their East European client states. Great numbers of people rose up nonviolently, Christians and churches had a crucial role, and (except in Romania) repressive governments were toppled by these nonviolent uprisings.

Those amazing events in 1989 relate very much to another standard question: "But what about Hitler?" A similar attitude was expressed to me with deep emotion some years ago by a young mother as she held a child: "I would rather he'd be killed than for him to live under Communism." That was her equivalent of "better dead than Red," better dead in a nuclear war than alive under Communist rule.

Yet for Czechs, Hungarians, and Poles to live under Communist governments has so clearly been immensely better than to have had a nuclear war devastating their countries and much of the world. And the time came when enough courage and will emerged among these populations to make possible the nonviolent overthrow of the Communist regimes.

The gigantic military forces of the United States and its continuing reliance on nuclear weapons do not really defend us. All of that still puts us in considerable danger of war and, in any case, brings with it vast social deterioration, hardness of heart, and misery in this country and around the world. Too often Christian disciples have given in to the way of war and preparations for war. But from Jesus we know that the military way is a dead end and cannot truly defend those it is intended to defend. That is also pragmatically true.

George Kennan and some other analysts were saying for decades that the posture of the Soviet Union was defensive and fearful and not oriented toward taking over the rest of the world. As we saw in 1989, the Soviet government decided not to pay the price of military intervention to keep its hold in Eastern Europe. Clearly, the Soviets had no intention and no real capability of conquering and occupying the United States.

We don't need a $300-billion-a-year military establishment to prevent such a conquest. Suppose Americans generally would have the same readiness to rise up in nonviolent resistance as did the East Germans and the Czechs. Then any country seen as the enemy would find it impossible to establish and maintain control over a population as large as that of the United States.

Ponder another standard comment: "We have to be realistic"; in the real world we have to be ready to fight and go to war. But for us as Christians, Jesus Christ is the central reality in history, and from him we discern what is realistic, what is in conformity to him. Doing that, we disengage ourselves from the web of nationalist militarism and violence ensnaring our country and world. We give ourselves to peacemaking, imaginative initiatives toward reconciliation, and readiness to defend nonviolently those whom we love.

The way of violence and war involves great risks. The loving, nonviolent way of Jesus involves great risks. But with Jesus, we can face and meet the risks of nonviolence. This Lord calls us to say NO! to the military and to live his love for all the human family.

This essay by Dale Aukerman (see page 77) is adapted from the *Peace Studies Bulletin* of Manchester College. Used by permission. Dale Aukerman is the author of *Darkening Valley* (Scottdale, Pa.: Herald Press, 1989 reprint) and *Dawn at Midnight: Terminal Politics and Messianic Hope* (New York: Crossroad and Continuum, 1993).

BUT DOES IT REALLY WORK?

As section 1 already pointed out, the Christian does not choose a nonviolent approach to conflict because of assurance it will always work. The Christian chooses that approach because of commitment to the lordship of Jesus Christ.

Yet we can also ask the practical question: Does it work? The answer: Yes, often.

While we do not have assurance that the soft answer will *always* turn away wrath, we do know it often does. There are enough reports of incidents even in recent times to convince us of that.

Ten stories follow. These, and many more which could be added to them, show that nonviolence, given a chance, has more to offer to a conflict situation than the reflex appeal to violence.

Something or Somebody Glued Them

by Tom Skinner

At the very moment Jesus Christ came into my life, I saw no blinding flashes of light. I heard no thunder roar. I simply accepted the fact that if God was God, then God could only be God because he does not lie. Jesus Christ took up residence in my life and has been living in me ever since.

The following night, I faced my entire gang, the Harlem Lords—129 guys with knives and pistols and no reservations about using them. I told them I had committed my life to Christ and based on that commitment, could no longer lead the gang.

All the time I was talking, something inside of me was saying, "Cat, you is a fool! You ain't getting out of here alive!" Sitting in front of me was the No. 2 man in the gang. His nickname was the "Mop" because he was never happy in a fight unless he drew blood from someone and then put his foot in it.

I knew that he wanted to be No. 1 man, and I also knew he would say my committing my life to Christ was a sign of weakness. But I walked out. Not one of those guys moved.

Two nights later the "Mop" cornered me and said, "Tom,

the other night when you walked out, I was going to put my blade in your back, but I couldn't move. It was like something or somebody glued me to my seat." He said the other fellows told him the same thing.

Then I knew that the Christ to whom I had committed myself was more than just some fictitious character who lived 1,900 years ago or some nebulous spirit floating around in space somewhere—he was alive and real.

I asked the "Mop" if he would like to know that person who kept him glued to his seat, and he said, "Yes." Standing right there on the street corner, the No. 2 man bowed his head and invited Jesus Christ into his life.

Until the events recounted here, Tom Skinner was gang leader of the Harlem Lords. His agency, Tom Skinner Crusades, has for over a decade been America's major black-led evangelistic agency. The excerpt is taken from the book *Black and Free* by Tom Skinner, copyright © 1968 by Zondervan Publishing House. Used by permission.

by
an
anonymous
missionary

It Was Like a Spring Thaw

The Japanese troops approached the abandoned American university a couple of miles outside the little Chinese village. Morgan, the lone American missionary, could hear the menacing rattle of machine guns in the distance, but he decided to stand his ground at the gate of the institution where he had taught until the invasion drove the school westward.

They came along the road—dirty, disheveled, tense, and utterly weary. "As tired looking a bunch of men as I've ever seen," Morgan thought. It was a small contingent, a sort of advance guard. They would trot along the road a hundred yards and then squat down, set up a machine gun, and spray the road ahead. They paid little attention to the man standing by the gate as they went by.

By the next day the nearby village had become a field headquarters for the Japanese, and Morgan's tribulations began. As he had anticipated, the Japanese officers cast covetous glances at the university buildings. Soon a group of them called on Morgan and demanded the keys.

The missionary declined, politely but firmly. He explained that the property belonged to American mission boards, that it had been entrusted to his care, and that he was not at liberty to hand it over to anyone else. An hour and a half of discussion, with the missionary remaining always courteous and friendly but firm, convinced the Japanese, and they left.

Unfortunately, that was not the end. Periodically, on an average of every two weeks, the village garrison changed, and each new contingent had to be persuaded all over again. Through it all Morgan did his best to remain calm and friendly.

But then came a major crisis. This time something had happened to make the Japanese less patient, less willing to listen to the missionary's arguments. Morgan sensed the tension in the air immediately. He could not help reflecting that, isolated as he was, the Japanese could do with him as they would. No "neutral" witnesses could be summoned to testify against them. A dead missionary could easily be explained by a "stray bullet—so sorry!"

Nevertheless, he greeted them cordially, as always, and refused their request for the keys of the building with his usual regretful firmness. This time, though, the most eloquent arguments appeared only to inflame the soldiers more. Finally the officer in command of the detachment delivered an ultimatum.

"Surrender the keys," he demanded flatly, "or we shoot you!"

The missionary stood a little straighter. "I have told you how it is," he replied quietly. "I wish you no harm, but I cannot do what you ask. I cannot."

Grimly the officer counted off three men and lined them up facing the missionary.

"Ready!" he commanded, and rifles were raised to shoulders. He turned to the missionary. "Surrender the keys!"

"I cannot. I have told you I cannot. I have no hatred

against you. I have only the friendliest feelings for you. But I cannot give you the keys."

Morgan thought he could see admiration in the soldiers' eyes—admiration and baffled wonderment, as though they could not understand what held him erect and smiling in the very face of death.

Later he said, "I felt no fear. I was perfectly calm. My only prayer was for enough love to disarm my attackers. I tried to show them—the men as well as their officers—that I had in fact the friendliest feelings for them, that I recognized them as brothers and would refuse to cooperate with them only when they wished me to do something wrong. I tried to put that into my eyes as well as into my words."

"Aim!" The officer's voice was gruff as he turned once more to the missionary. "Your last chance," he said. "Surrender the keys!"

There was a pause. Morgan looked directly at the men who stood with leveled rifles facing him. He spoke to them, as one man to other men, as brother to brother.

"I cannot," he said. "You know that I cannot."

The stillness was absolute. The missionary looked steadily at the men. The officer seemed uncertain, the men uneasy. Then, one at a time, they relaxed. Rifles lowered; sheepish grins replaced their looks of grim determination.

But the danger had not passed. One man of the firing squad apparently was disgusted and embarrassed at the outcome of this situation. He gripped his rifle and glared at Morgan.

"Father," the missionary prayed, "a little more love. Let me show a little more love."

The soldier had decided. Abruptly, with fixed bayonet on the end of his rifle, he launched himself full tilt at the missionary.

"He came fast," Morgan recalls, "and he came hard. At the last instant, when the point of his bayonet was not a foot from me, I dodged. He missed, and the force of his charge carried him up to me. I reached around him and with my right hand grabbed the butt of his rifle. (I thought that under the circumstances even a pacifist might be forgiven for holding a rifle!) With my left hand I grasped him around the shoulders (and that was a pretty hefty grip, too, for a pacifist) and pulled him tight up against me. I was taller than he, and he had to look up at me. When our eyes met, his face was contorted with fury.

"Our glances locked and held for seconds that seemed ages long. Then I smiled down at him, and it was like a spring thaw melting the ice on a frozen river. The hatred vanished and, after a sheepish moment, he smiled back!"

That was the end. A few minutes later the soldiers, like a group of bewildered children, were trailing the missionary into his living quarters—to have tea before their tiring journey back to the village.

The American Protestant missionary recounting this experience was a member of the Fellowship of Reconciliation, in whose journal, *Fellowship*, it first appeared in the January 1945 issue. Reprinted by permission.

by
Gladys
Aylward,
as told to
Alan
Burgess

You Say You Have the Living God Inside You

"What's the paper for, anyway?" she asked Lu-Yung-Cheng.

"It's an official summons from the *yamen*," said Lu-Yung-Cheng nervously. "A riot has broken out in the men's prison."

Gladys was really not very interested. "Oh, has it?" she said.

"You must come at once," said the messenger urgently. "It is most important!"

Gladys stared at him. "But what's the riot in the prison got to do with us? It can't have anything to do with my foot-inspection."*

"You must come at once!" reiterated the messenger loudly. "It is an official order." He hopped from one foot to the other in impatience.

---

*Gladys had been authorized by the provincial governor of Yang-cheng in northern China to implement a new law forbidding the binding of the feet of young girls.

Lu-Yung-Cheng looked at her doubtfully. "When that piece of red paper arrives from the *yamen*, you must go." There was a nervous tremor in his voice.

"All right, *you* go and see what it's all about," said Gladys. "It's obviously a man's job. I know nothing about prisons. I've never been in one in my life. Though I really don't see what you're supposed to do."

She could see from Lu-Yung-Cheng's face that the prospect did not appeal to him.

"Hurry, please hurry!" cried the messenger.

Reluctantly, Lu-Yung-Cheng trailed after him to the door. Gladys watched him reach the opening, take a quick look behind at her, then dodge swiftly to the left as the messenger turned to the right. She could hear the sound of his feet running as he tore down the road.

Within two seconds the messenger discovered his loss. He stormed back through the doorway crying "Ai-ee-ee!" and shaking his fist in rage. He raced across the courtyard toward Gladys, a little fat man without dignity.

"Now *you* must come," he shouted. "This is an official paper. You are ordered to come. You *must* come. Now! With me! If you refuse you will get into trouble!"

"All right," she said mildly. "I'll come. I really don't know what's the matter with Lu-Yung-Cheng. He must feel ill or something. But I certainly don't see what a riot in the prison has to do with me."

They hurried up the road and in through the east gate. A few yards inside the gate the blank outside wall of the prison flanked the main street. From the other side came an unholy cacophony: screams, shouts, yells, the most horrible noises.

"My goodness!" said Gladys, "it certainly is a riot, isn't it?"

The governor of the prison, small, pale-faced, his mouth

set into a worried line, met her at the entrance. Behind were grouped half a dozen of his staff.

"We are glad you have come," he said quickly. "There is a riot in the prison; the convicts are killing each other."

"So I can hear," she said. "But what am I here for? I'm only the missionary woman. Why don't you send the soldiers in to stop it?"

"The convicts are murderers, bandits, thieves," said the governor, his voice trembling. "The soldiers are frightened. There are not enough of them."

"I'm sorry to hear that," said Gladys. "But what do you expect me to do about it? I don't even know why you asked me to come."

The governor took a step forward. "You must go in and stop the fighting!"

"I must go in...!" Gladys's mouth dropped open; her eyes rounded in utter amazement. "Me! Me go in there! Are you mad! If I went in, they'd kill me!"

The governor's eyes were fixed on her with hypnotic intensity. "But how can they kill you? You tell everybody that you have come here because you have the living God inside you."

The words bubbled out of the governor's mouth, his lips twisted in the acuteness of distress. Gladys felt a small, cold shiver down her back. When she swallowed, her throat seemed to have a gritty texture.

"The—living God?" she stammered.

"You preach it everywhere—in the streets and villages. If you preach the truth, if your God protects you from harm, then you can stop this riot."

Gladys stared at him. Her mind raced round in bewilderment, searching for some fact that would explain her beliefs to this simple, deluded man. A little cell in her mind kept blinking on and off with an urgent semaphore message: "It's true! You have been preaching that your Christian God protects you from harm. Fail now, and you are finished in Yangcheng. Discard your faith now, and you discard it for ever!"

It was a desperate challenge. Somehow she had to maintain face. Oh, these stupidly simple people! But how could she go into the prison? Those men—murderers, thieves, bandits, rioting and killing each other inside those walls! By the sounds, louder now, a small human hell had broken loose. How could she . . . ? "I must try," she said to herself. "I must try. O God, give me strength."

She looked up at the governor's pale face, knowing that now hers was the same color. "All right," she said. "Open the door. I'll go in to them." She did not trust her voice to say any more.

"The key!" snapped the governor. "The key, quickly."

One of his orderlies came forward with a huge iron key. It looked designed to unlock the deepest, darkest dungeon in the world. In the keyhole it grated loudly; the immense iron-barred door swung open. Literally she was pushed inside. It was dark. The door closed behind her. She heard the great key turn.

She was locked in the prison with a horde of raving criminals who by their din sounded as if they had all gone completely insane. A dark tunnel, twenty yards long, stretched before her. At the far end it appeared to open out into a courtyard. She could see figures racing across the entrance. With faltering footsteps, she walked through it and came to an abrupt standstill, rooted in horror.

The courtyard was about sixty feet square with queer cage-like structures round all four sides. Within its confines a writhing, fiendish battle was going on. Several bodies were stretched out on the flagstones. One man, obviously dead, lay only a few feet away from her, blood still pouring from a great wound in his scalp. There was blood everywhere. Inside the cage-like structures small private battles were being fought.

The main group of men, however, were watching one convict who brandished a large, blood-stained chopper. As she stared, he suddenly rushed at them, and they scattered wildly to every part of the square. Gladys stood there, aghast at this macabre form of "tag." The man on the ground with the gash in his skull had obviously been well and truly "tagged."

No one took any notice whatsoever of Gladys. For fully half a minute she stood motionless with not one single cell of her mind operating to solve her dilemma. The man rushed again; the group parted; he singled one man out and chased him. The man ran toward Gladys, then ducked away. The madman with the ax halted only a few feet from her. Without any instinctive plan, hardly realizing what she was doing, she took two angry steps toward him.

"Give me that chopper," she said furiously. "Give it to me at once!" The man turned to look at her. For three long seconds the wild dark pupils staring from bloodshot eyes glared at her. He took two paces forward. Suddenly, meekly, he held out the ax.

Gladys snatched the weapon from his hand and held it rigidly down by her side. She was conscious that there was blood on the blade and that it would stain her trousers. The other convicts—there must have been fifty or sixty men cowering there—stared from every corner of the courtyard. All action was frozen in that one moment of intense drama. Gladys knew that she must clinch her psychological advantage.

"All of you!" she shouted. "Come over here. Come on, form into a line!" She knew vaguely that the voice belonged to her, but she had never heard it so shrill. She screamed at them, gabbled at them like an undersized infuriated sergeant-major, like a schoolmarm with a class of naughty children. "Get into line at once. You, over there! Come on, form up in front of me!"

Obediently the convicts shambled across, forming into a ragged group before her. She regarded them stormily. There was silence. Then suddenly her fear had gone. In its place was an immense, soul-searing pity that pricked the tears into her eyes. They were so wretched. They were so hopeless. A mass of thin faces: angular cheekbones, puckered lips; faces contorted with misery, pain, and hunger; eyes, dark with fear and despair, that looked into hers.

They were remnants of humanity, half-men dressed in rags, caked in dust, running with lice; animals more than men, and the cages in which they were penned around the arena were those of brutes. She could have wept openly that human creatures could be so wretched. With an effort she tightened her lips and took command again. The fear had gone, yes; but she knew she must still cow them with her authority.

"You should be ashamed of yourselves," she said, berating them like an irate mother scolding a crowd of naughty children. "All this noise and all this mess!" Mess! She waved her arms to indicate the bodies and blood the battle had left behind. "The governor sent me in here to find out what it was all about. Now, if you clean up this courtyard and promise to behave in future, I'll ask him to deal leniently with you this time."

She tried to keep her eyes away from the still figures of the dead. She knew she must focus their attention until all the desperate violence had seeped away. "Now, what is your grievance?" she snapped. "Why did you start fighting like this?"

There was no answer. Several hung their heads in shame.

"I want you to appoint a spokesman, then," she went on. "He can tell me what the trouble is. And then you can start cleaning up this courtyard at once. Now go over in that corner and appoint your spokesman. I'll wait here."

The convicts trooped over into the corner she indicated and talked among themselves. A few moments later, one of the taller men of slightly better physique approached. Like the others, he was dressed in rags.

"My name is Feng," he said. "I am their spokesman."

While they swabbed up the blood with rags, and moved the dead bodies into less spectacular positions, Gladys listened to his story. Later she learned that he had once been a Buddhist priest; he had been convicted of theft from the other priests of the temple and sentenced to eight years in jail. He explained that no one really knew why, or how, the riot had started. They were allowed the chopper—he indicated the ax which Gladys still carried—for an hour every day to cut up their food. Someone had quarreled over its possession, someone else had joined in, and suddenly, without anyone knowing exactly why, the volcano of passion had erupted and a lava of blood flowed everywhere.

He could not explain this strange occurrence. Perhaps it was that many of the men had been there for many years, he said. As she knew, unless their friends or relatives sent in food, they starved. It was hard to sit up against a wall and starve to death while other men ate. Sometimes they took one of their number out into the square and executed him. That terror hung over many heads. He could not explain the outbreak, but the walls were high and the doors were strong;

they never saw the outside world, women or the mountains, a tree in blossom or a friendly face; sometimes the spirit grew so oppressed that it burst out of a man in a wild tumult of violence. That, he thought, is what had occurred. They were all very sorry.

"What do you do all day in here?" asked Gladys seriously.

"Do? There is nothing to do."

"No occupation of any sort?"

"None!"

"But a man must have work, something to do. I shall see the governor about it."

It was at that moment she became conscious that the governor and his retinue were behind her. She did not find out until later that there was a small opening toward the end of the tunnel through which they had heard everything. The noise of the riot had died, and they had now thought it safe to enter and take an official part in the peace treaty.

The governor bowed to Gladys.

"You have done well," he said gratefully. "We must thank you."

"It's disgraceful," she said bitterly. "These men are locked up here week after week, year after year, with nothing to do. Nothing to do at all!"

"I do not understand." His bewilderment was rather ludicrous.

Gladys could, however, sense his gratitude and decided to press her point. "Of course you have riots if they've nothing to occupy their time year after year. You must find them occupations."

The governor was still completely puzzled. "Occupations?" he repeated.

"They must have work to do. We must get looms so they can weave cloth; we must find them all sorts of jobs so that they can earn a little money and buy food and get back a little self-respect."

The governor nodded. Whether he agreed or not she could not tell. "We will discuss it later," he said amiably.

"I have promised them there will be no reprisals," she said.

The governor nodded again. A few corpses were rarely the subject of an official inquiry or even an embarrassment to the Chinese penal system. "As long as there is no recurrence," he said, "we shall forget all about it."

"That is good," said Gladys. She turned to Feng. "I'm going now, but I shall come back. I promise I will do all I can to help you."

She saw upon her the dark eyes of the priest who was a thief. "Thank you," he said. "Thank you, Ai-weh-deh."

She did not know at the time what the word "Ai-weh-deh" meant. That evening she asked Lu-Yung-Cheng when he returned from the long walk he had so suddenly decided to take.

"Ai-weh-deh?" he said curiously. "It means the virtuous one."

She was known as Ai-weh-deh for all her remaining years in China.

Gladys Aylward was an independent British missionary in Yangcheng, south of Peking, China, from 1930 to 1941. Her true experience has been fictionalized in the film "The Inn of the Sixth Happiness," with Ingrid Bergman playing the role based on Miss Aylward. Reprinted from *The Small Woman* by Alan Burgess (London: Evans Brothers, Ltd., 1957) by permission of Bell & Hyman, Ltd.

by
Terry
Dobson

The Art of Reconciliation

The train clanked and rattled through the suburbs of Tokyo on a drowsy spring afternoon. Our car was comparatively empty—a few housewives with their kids in tow, some old folks going shopping. I gazed absently at the drab houses and dusty hedgerows.

At one station the doors opened, and suddenly the afternoon quiet was shattered by a man bellowing violent, incomprehensible curses. The man staggered into our car. He wore laborer's clothing, and he was big, drunk, and dirty. Screaming, he swung at a woman holding a baby. The blow sent her spinning into the laps of an elderly couple. It was a miracle that the baby was unharmed.

Terrified, the couple jumped up and scrambled toward the other end of the car. The laborer aimed a kick at the retreating back of the old woman but missed as she scuttled to safety. This so enraged the drunk that he grabbed the metal pole in the center of the car and tried to wrench it out of its stanchion. I could see that one of his hands was cut and bleeding. The train lurched ahead, the passengers frozen with fear. I stood up.

I was young then, some 20 years ago, and in pretty good shape. I'd been putting in a solid eight hours of aikido training nearly every day for the past three years. I liked to throw and grapple. I thought I was tough. Trouble was, my martial skill was untested in actual combat. As students of aikido, we were not allowed to fight.

"Aikido," my teacher had said again and again, "is the art of reconciliation. Whoever has the mind to fight has broken his connection with the universe. If you try to dominate people, you are already defeated. We study how to resolve conflict, not how to start it."*

I had listened to his words. I had tried hard. I even went so far as to cross the street to avoid the *chimpira*, the pinball punks who lounged around the train stations. My forbearance exalted me. I felt both tough and holy. In my heart, however, I wanted an absolutely legitimate opportunity whereby I might save the innocent by destroying the guilty.

This is it! I said to myself as I got to my feet. *People are in danger. If I don't do something fast, somebody will probably get hurt.*

Seeing me stand up, the drunk recognized a chance to focus his rage. "Aha!" he roared. "A foreigner! You need a lesson in Japanese manners!"

I held on lightly to the commuter strap overhead and gave him a slow look of disgust and dismissal. I planned to take this turkey apart, but he had to make the first move. I wanted him mad, so I pursed my lips and blew him an insolent kiss.

"All right!" he hollered. "You're gonna get a lesson." He gathered himself for a rush at me.

A split second before he could move, someone shouted

---

*Aikido is a Japanese art of settling conflicts using holds, locks, and throws resembling those of judo and jujitsu.

"Hey!" It was earsplitting. I remember the strangely joyous, lilting quality of it—as though you and a friend had been searching diligently for something, and he had suddenly stumbled upon it. "Hey!"

I wheeled to my left; the drunk spun to his right. We both stared down at a little old Japanese. He must have been well into his seventies, this tiny gentleman, sitting there immaculate in his kimono. He took no notice of me but beamed delightedly at the laborer, as though he had a most important, most welcome secret to share.

"C'mere," the old man said in an easy vernacular, beckoning to the drunk. "C'mere and talk with me." He waved his hand lightly.

The big man followed, as if on a string. He planted his feet belligerently in front of the old gentleman and roared above the clacking wheels, "Why the hell should I talk to you?" The drunk now had his back to me. If his elbow moved so much as a millimeter, I'd drop him in his socks.

The old man continued to beam at the laborer. "What'cha been drinkin'?" he asked, his eyes sparkling with interest.

"I been drinkin' sake," the laborer bellowed back, "and it's none of your business!" Flecks of spittle spattered the old man.

"Oh, that's wonderful," the old man said, "absolutely wonderful! You see, I love sake too. Every night, me and my wife (she's 76, you know), we warm up a little bottle of sake and take it out into the garden, and we sit on an old wooden bench. We watch the sun go down, and we look to see how our persimmon tree is doing. My great-grandfather planted that tree, and we worry about whether it will recover from those ice storms we had last winter. Our tree has done better than I expected, though, especially when you consider the poor quality of the soil. It is gratifying to watch when we take our sake and go out to enjoy the evening—even when it rains!'' He looked up at the laborer, eyes twinkling.

As he struggled to follow the old man's conversation, the drunk's face began to soften. His fists slowly unclenched. "Yeah, I love persimmons too. . . " his voice trailed off.

"Yes," said the old man, smiling, "and I'm sure you have a wonderful wife."

"No," replied the laborer. "My wife died." Very gently, swaying with the motion of the train, the big man began to sob. "I don't got no *wife*, I don't got no *home*, I don't got no *job*. I'm so *ashamed* of myself." Tears rolled down his cheeks; a spasm of despair rippled through his body.

Now it was my turn. Standing there in my well-scrubbed youthful innocence, my make-this-world-safe-for-democracy righteousness, I suddenly felt dirtier than he was.

Then the train arrived at my stop. As the doors opened, I heard the old man cluck sympathetically. "My, my," he said, "that is a difficult predicament indeed. Sit down here and tell me about it."

I turned my head for one last look. The laborer was sprawled on the seat, his head on the old man's lap. The old man was softly stroking the filthy, matted hair.

As the train pulled away, I sat down on a bench. What I had wanted to do with muscle had been accomplished with kind words. I had just seen aikido tried in combat, and the essence of it was love. I would have to practice the art with an entirely different spirit. It would be a long time before I could speak about the resolution of conflict.

Reprinted by permission of the author from *Reader's Digest* where it appeared in the December 1981 issue under the title, "A Soft Answer."

Sometimes What It Takes Is Trust

by Dorothy T. Samuel

In 1972 two quite ordinary young women in Philadelphia walked out one night to pay their rent. They carried neither bag nor purse. After paying the rent, they drifted home penniless, rather obviously penniless. Yet on the dark, empty city street, they were suddenly confronted by a tall youth who held a knife to the throat of the one nearer him.

"I want money. I have to have money."

It does happen on the streets today—the pain-crazed junkie desperate for a "fix." And, having made an approach, quiet retreat becomes for him the certainty of sudden chase by alerted police with screaming sirens and flashing lights and unholstered guns. The stickup is not a business where one can turn from a poor prospect and calmly seek a more promising customer.

What should the two women do? Were either to flee, they recognized at once, the other would fall to the knife.

"I don't want to do this," the junkie said. "I don't like to hurt people. But sometimes I have to!" The knife moved closer. "And if I have to, I will now. If I don't get money, someone is going to get hurt."

"But we don't have any money!"

"I have to have money!"

They began thinking of alternatives for him. None of them would do.

"If I don't get money, you'll get hurt."

"Look," said the smaller one, chin firm over the knife, "I'll stay here with you. Let Mary go back to my apartment and get you the money."

"No way! She'll call the cops."

"No, she won't! Really she won't. And I'll be here. She wouldn't call the cops while I was still here."

Still no one on the street. The three stood in an intimate little drama, knife blackened to avoid the light. A strange understanding began to grow in the young women. He really *didn't* like to do this. He really *was* miserable. He was also irrational. And more frightened, really, than they.

"Look, you come back with us. I have some money in my apartment. You come with us."

"No! Your husband will be there. Some man will be there." The jerky threat of the knife again.

"There's no one there. Honestly. The apartment is empty. Look, trust us. We'll get you the money."

"You'll call the fuzz."

"Trust us. Come on, we'll all go."

"It's a trick."

"It's no trick."

Was he weakening? His position was as futile as theirs— more futile. They simply had no money to give him there on the street. Bluster as he might, he could not make them produce what they did not have. And hurting them would not really help. He was in an impossible situation, and that terrible futility added to his crazed frustration.

"Look, trust us." She spoke to him directly, person to person—looked him in the eye, one human to another. "I live just at the corner. Come along to the apartment."

He was wavering.

"There is no one there. Trust us. Come on."

Slowly, knife at the ready, he began to move along the dark street with them. The young woman kept talking quietly, normally.

At the outer door, he pulled her nearer to the knife.

"Just upstairs. There's no one there. Just trust us."

Inside the foyer. Up the stairs. Key in the lock. And the other young woman took over the position under the knife while the smaller one went into her apartment and rummaged for her purse. Ten dollars. A ten-dollar bill was all the money she had. She ran back to the door, thrust it at him.

"Is that all you have?"

A sudden sinking feeling. After all this, after the appearance of trust, the seeming solution of their predicament, was he going to demand more? She had no more. And her apartment door stood open behind her.

"That's all. That's really all."

"But I only need five dollars. I don't have change."

"Take it. Take it. That's all right."

"But I only need five." His hands were shaking, his voice trembling.

"That's all right. Take it. Take it."

He looked down at the bill, back into the young woman's eyes.

"Bye," she said. "Bye now."

And he slithered down the steps and out into the night.

Dorothy T. Samuel, commentator on WBAL-TV (Baltimore) and member of the English curriculum committee of the Baltimore public schools, is an advocate of Christian nonviolence. This excerpt is adapted from her book, *Safe Passage on City Streets*, copyright © 1975 by Dorothy T. Samuel. Used by permission of the publisher, Abingdon Press.

Welcoming the Enemy

by Sarah Corson

It was midnight. Before retiring I walked out on the screened porch where my 15-year-old son was sleeping. I was leading a team of 17 young people, including two of my own children, on a three-month work assignment in a jungle area 200 miles from the nearest city in a South American country. Four years before, my husband and I with our four children had first come to this area at the request of the village people to help them start a church, build a fish hatchery, and develop other forms of appropriate technology to meet basic human needs. After the church and appropriate technology center had been established we moved to work in another country. This summer the village had asked us to return to experiment with a vegetable protein project.

When we received the invitation, my husband was already committed to a project in Haiti for the summer. We decided to divide up for three months in order to work in both projects. My husband took our 14-year-old Karen with him to Haiti while our 15-year-old Tommy and 16-year-old Kathy went with me, leaving our 19-year-old Chris to take care of things at our headquarters in Alabama.

The air on the porch was chilly, so I laid a blanket across Tommy's cot, then stood a moment looking out across the

fishponds that were bringing hope for more food to our
village. The light from the moon made a rippling path of
white across the water.

Suddenly I heard a crash. Turning quickly I could see in
the moonlight that a soldier had slid into our water barrel. I
was paralyzed with shock as I looked out over the clearing
that separated our temporary home from the jungle. About
30 soldiers were rushing our house.

Our host country had just held elections, not the usual
custom, and the military did not agree with the results. It
had taken over one week before, exiling the newly elected
president and repressing any resistance, real or imagined.
Since we were in such a remote frontier village, I had not expected the fighting to reach us.

While I stood there, frozen in fear, watching the soldiers
surround our house, the message a neighbor woman had
brought me that day flashed through my mind.

"Sister, keep your team in the house," she had urged. "I
just came from the market over near the military camp. I
overheard two soldiers saying the Americans were to blame
for the resistance to their takeover. They said they would not
rest until they had exterminated every American in this
zone."

Since we had not been involved in political activities in
their country, I thought that she had misunderstood. I did
not think that we would be suspected of participating in
such resistance, but now what the neighbor woman had
warned me about was taking place before my eyes. Evi-
dently, the soldiers were intent on carrying out their threat.
If they wanted to kill us, there was no way we could stop
them.

My heart was beating so fast, I thought my blood vessels
would burst. It felt as if I was about to have a stroke. I knew

I had a responsibility for the team members inside the house, but I could not even call out to them. I was paralyzed with fear.

I had only a split second to pray before the soldiers found me: "God, if I have to die, take care of my family. And God, please take away this fear. I don't want to die afraid. Please help me to die trusting you." I was suddenly aware of the presence of God.

We do not always feel God. Usually we trust God by faith. However, at that moment God's presence was very real, seemingly touchable. I still thought I was going to die, but I knew God had things under control. I remember thinking that maybe our deaths would accomplish things that we had not been able to accomplish with our lives.

I found myself stepping up to the closest soldier and speaking words I could never have thought to say. "Welcome, brother," I called out. "Come in. You do not need guns to visit us."

At that the soldier jumped, dropped the bullet he was putting in his gun, and shouted, "Not me. I'm not the one. I'm just following orders. There's the commander over there, he's the one."

I raised my voice and repeated, "You're all welcome. Everyone is welcome in our home."

At that the commander ran up to me, shoved the muzzle of his rifle against my stomach, and pushed me through the door into the house. Thirty soldiers rushed into the house and began pulling everything off the shelves and out of drawers, looking for guns. They herded the team members into the kitchen, where they sat quietly by the glow of the two candles we used for light.

The soldier who led the attack turned his gun on me and demanded angrily, "What are you Americans doing down here—trying to stop our revolution? Seventeen Americans would not be living in this poverty if they did not have political motivation."

"Sir," I responded truthfully, "we have had nothing to do with your revolution. We are here for two reasons. We are teaching self-help projects to the hungry and we are teaching the Bible."

"That tells me nothing," he responded. "I have never read the Bible in my life. Maybe it is a communist book, for all I know."

"You have never read the Bible in your life? Oh, sir, I am so sorry for you. You have missed the best part of your life. Please let me tell you what it says."

He made no objection. He had to stand there with his gun on us while the other soldiers ransacked the house looking for the guns we did not have.

I picked up a Spanish Bible and turned to the Sermon on the Mount. "We teach about Jesus Christ," I said, "God's Son who came into this world to save us. He also taught us a better way than fighting. He taught us the way of love. Because of him I can tell you that even though you kill me, I will die loving you because God loves you. To follow him, I have to love you too."

In that particular Bible there were paragraph captions. He glanced at them and read plainly, "Jesus teaches love your enemies," and "Return good for evil."

"That's humanly impossible!" he burst out.

"That's true, sir," I answered. "It isn't humanly possible, but with God's help it is possible."

"I don't believe it."

"You can prove it, sir. I know you came here to kill us. So just kill me slowly, if you want to prove it. Cut me to pieces little by little, and you will see you cannot make me hate you. I will die praying for you because God loves you, and we love you too."

The soldier lowered his gun and stepped back. Clearing his throat, he said, "You almost convince me you are innocent—but I have orders to take everyone in the house and the ham radio. I will let you get some warm clothes and a blanket—you will be sleeping on the ground."

They marched us two by two at gunpoint down a trail to where a truck was waiting on the one little road that came into our village. We saw that others in our town had been taken prisoner also. The district superintendent of the church, the leader of the youth group, and other leaders were lined up at gunpoint, ready to be loaded on the trucks with us.

Suddenly the soldier changed his mind: "Halt!" he said. "Take only the men. The women will come with me."

He led us back to our home, saying, "I don't know why I am doing this. I was about to take you into a jungle camp of over a thousand soldiers. I know what they do to women prisoners. You would be abused many times. I cannot take you.

"In our army no one breaks an order," he continued sternly. "I have never broken an order before, but for the first time tonight I am refusing to obey an order. If my superior officer finds out that you were in this house when I raided it, and that I did not take you, I will pay for it with my life." He strode to the door, stopped, and looked back again.

"I could have fought any amount of guns you might have had," he said, "but there is something here I cannot understand. I cannot fight it."

Then the hard part began—waiting to hear what had happened to the men of our team and the leaders of the village. The waiting, the uncertainty, seemed endless. If a twig snapped outside our window everyone jumped, thinking the soldiers were back again. The people of our village were as distressed as we were. They stood around in our house all day—some weeping, others coming to offer their sympathy. No one knew what would happen next.

The local people insisted we could not have a service in the church on Sunday because the soldiers considered any meeting held to be for the purpose of political agitation. "Soldiers will be there if you have a service. They will take more prisoners," they told me. We all agreed to pray at home on Sunday.

But on Saturday night a messenger came to our door. "I bring a message from the man who commanded the attack on your village Thursday night," he said. "He says he will be at your service Sunday. However, he has no vehicle on Sundays so you are to bring the church's jeep and get him. He said to tell you that if you don't come he will be there anyway, even if he has to walk the 10 miles." It sounded like a threat.

I sent a message to everyone in the town that night. "We will have the service after all," I told them, "but you are not obligated to come. In fact you may lose your life by coming. No one knows what this soldier will do. Do not come when the church bell rings unless you are sure God wants you to come." I knew that the villagers feared the military and stayed out of sight when soldiers were around. I did not expect any of them to come.

The next morning I took the jeep and went to get the commander. He came with a bodyguard. The two of them marched coldly into the church and sat down, still holding their rifles. The women on our team came in, the bell was rung, and we began to sing. The church was packed before the first hymn was over. The people came pale and trembling, but they came. They had felt that their faith was at stake, and they were determined to attend, even if it meant imprisonment.

Since the leaders of the church had been taken by the military, I led the service. I tried to do just what I would have done had the soldiers not been there. It was church custom to welcome visitors by inviting them to the platform, singing a welcome song, and waving to them. Everyone would then line up to shake the visitors' hands, hug them, and say some personal words of greeting.

How could I ask these people to hug the very man who had taken their husband, son, or brother prisoner? That was asking too much. I decided that I would ask them to sing a welcome song but that I would stop there and leave out the hugging.

The soldiers were surprised when I asked them to come to the platform to let us welcome them. "Welcome us?" they asked in amazement. "Well, all right," they shrugged. They came forward and stood very formally with their guns across their backs.

The people stood, singing weakly and waving their hands timidly. I expected them to sit back down, but no. The first man on the front seat came forward and put out his hand. As he bent over to hug the soldier I heard him say, "Brother, we don't like what you did to our village, but this is the house of God, and God loves you, so you are welcome here."

Everyone in the church followed his example, even the women whose eyes were red from weeping for their loved ones whom this man had taken prisoner. They too said words of welcome. The looks on the soldiers' faces became ones of surprise, then incredulity.

When the last person finished greeting them, the head

soldier marched to the pulpit and said in a very stern voice, "Now I will have a few words. Never have I ever dreamed that I could raid a town, come back, and have that town welcome me as a brother. I can hardly believe what I have seen and heard this morning. That sister told me Thursday night that Christians love their enemies, but I did not believe her then. You have proven it to me this morning," he said to the congregation.

"This is the first church service I have ever been to," he continued. "I never believed there was a God before, but what I have just felt is so strong that I will never doubt the existence of God again as long as I live."

He turned from one side of the congregation to the other. "Do all of you know God?" he asked. "If you know God, hang on to him. It must be the greatest thing in this world to know God." As he spoke in an urgent voice he motioned with his hand, clenching it as though to hold on to something, while in his other hand he held a gun.

"I don't know God," he confessed in a low voice, "but I hope someday I shall, and that someday we can once again greet each other as brothers and sisters, as we have done this morning."

He came home with us for lunch. The men caught fish from the ponds to cook for his meal. The women helped me cook, even those who had lost a loved one. While we prepared lunch, the men took him around to see the brick project for dry housing, the chicken and vegetable protein project, and the clean water project. At last he said, "I have taken innocent people, but I did not know it when I did it. Now it is too late. If any of you need anything since you do not have your men, please tell me, and I will pay for it out of my pocket." He left, planning a return visit that was never to transpire.

Seven days later the bishop of our church sent a message for all Americans to come immediately to the capital city. He urged us to return to the United States as soon as possible, since he feared that our lives would be endangered by a possible countercoup.

Once in the capital, we learned that the American men who had been taken from our house at midnight had been taken by dump truck to a military camp 10 miles from our village. There they had been loaded on a plane with many other prisoners from the local area and flown to the capital, where they were held in a basement cell.

Three days later the U.S. embassy was successful in negotiating the release of the Americans and helping them leave the country. The local men, however, were not released for two weeks. Some, particularly the religious leaders, were tortured.

Often I think of the soldier and his 30 men who stormed out of the jungle ready to kill us. Within 15 minutes he had changed his mind and risked his life to save us. I thank God for putting divine love in my heart for a person I could not love on my own.

I cannot forget the last thing the soldier said to us as he left: "I have fought many battles and killed many people. It was nothing to me. It was just my job to exterminate them. But I never knew them personally. This is the first time I ever knew my enemy face to face, and I believe that if we knew each other, our guns would not be necessary."

Sarah Carson and her husband, Ken, are the founders of SIFAT (Servants in Faith and Technology), which offers practical training in meeting basic human needs. The group is located in Wedowee, Alabama. Reprinted with permission of the author from the April 1983 issue of *Sojourners*, P.O. Box 29272, Washington, D.C. 20017

by
Angie
O'Gorman

Defense Through Disarmament

Nonviolence and personal assault

Next to war, personal assault is one of the most terrifying experiences we encounter. Still, the faith questions must be asked. What does it mean to live out my belief in Gospel-based nonviolence when a man is standing in my bedroom? Ponder the Sermon on the Mount, the call to love enemies, and the centrality of reconciliation in the Christian ethic. Do these mean anything as I stand face-to-face with a burglar? A rapist? A man who may be a murderer?

Or is it better to say—as repeated for centuries in regard to war—that when the issue is defense from aggression, a different set of norms comes into play? The question takes on more urgency for those of us committed to disarmament between nations. If I believe disarmament is possible on the international level, how do I handle my own defense when personally threatened? How do I image my own preparedness? Are there alternatives to our culture-bound perceptions which equate defense with violence, and peace with passivity?

When defense is the issue, Westernized Christianity tends to define responsibility and right in terms of destroying whatever is experienced as threatening. In theological terms, we tend to see the destruction of evil as a necessary prelude to the coming of the kingdom of which Jesus spoke. Hence, if I kill or blind the rapist or render him sexually impaired, I have protected myself, bettered society, *and* furthered the coming of God's reign. Even if not said so bluntly, that is the logic. Destruction of evil is seen as the way to promote the good.

Examples of this rationale are not hard to find. Augustine included in his just-war theory the prohibition against killing a man unless you loved him. The motivation had to include the desire to save his soul. Yet even Augustine did not permit killing in self-defense. In his view, private citizens could not defend themselves by killing an aggressor because they could not do so without the loss of love. One could only kill in defense of the church or state. As this became the orthodox Catholic perspective, it merged with other theological understandings of the church's role as the keeper of God's law in the midst of an imperfect society. This role theologically legitimized killing in defense. In the Vietnam era, General Westmoreland used this same logic: "We had to destroy the village in order to save it."

It is hard to find a basis for this logic in the Scriptures. Rather than destruction of enemies, the Christian ethic calls for their conversion and counts on enough love on my part to facilitate the process. Somehow the oppressed, the victim, has a role to play in the life of the person held by evil—whether the roots of that evil are economic, psychological, or the effects of our cultural racism and sexism. Yet what can this mean for a person confronted by dangerous assaultive behavior? Not much, when there is no time for response in the interaction. With or without a gun, if you are clubbed on the head from behind, the chance for any defense is nil. But when the time sequence in an assault allows for defense, it allows for more than violence.

Jesus offered a different method of defense. He called it *love of enemies,* wanting wholeness, well-being, and life for those who may be broken, sick, and deadly (Matt. 5:44). Jesus meant this to be the cornerstone of an entirely new process of disarming evil, a response which would decrease evil instead of feeding it as violence does. In the context of assault, it means, among other things, to want safety for the assailant.

I agree that it sounds absurd, yet I have felt the power of that desire as a disarming force—not of an assailant, but of *myself.* I was awakened late one night several years ago by a man kicking open the door to my bedroom. The house was empty. The phone was downstairs. He was somewhat verbally abusive as he walked over to my bed. I could not find his eyes in the darkness but could see the outline of his form. As I lay there, feeling a fear and vulnerability I had never before experienced, several thoughts rushed through my head: First, the uselessness of screaming. Second, the fallacy of thinking safety depends on having a gun hidden under one's pillow. Somehow I could not imagine this man standing patiently while I reached under my pillow for my gun.

I believe the third thought saved my life. I realized with some clarity that either he and I made it through this situation safely—together—or we would both be damaged. Our safety was connected. If he raped me, I would be hurt both physically and emotionally, *and* he would be hurt as well. If he went to prison, the damage would be greater. That thought disarmed *me.* It also released me from paralysis and a desire to lash out. It freed me from fear's control over my ability to respond even though I still had feelings of fear. I found myself acting out of concern for the safety of us both, reacting with firmness but with little hostility in my voice.

I asked him what time it was. He answered. That was a good sign. I commented that his watch and the clock on my night table had different times. His said 2:30, mine said 2:45. I had just set mine. I hoped his watch wasn't broken. When had he last set it? He answered. I answered. The time seemed endless. When the atmosphere began to calm a little, I asked him how he had gotten into the house. He'd broken through the glass in the back door. I told him that presented me with a problem: I did not have the money to buy new glass. He talked about some financial difficulties of his own.

We talked until we were no longer strangers and I felt safe to ask him to leave. He didn't want to; he said he had no place to go. Knowing I did not have the physical power to force him out, I told him firmly but respectfully, as equal to equal, that I would give him a clean set of sheets, but he would have to make his own bed downstairs. He went downstairs, and I sat up in bed, wide awake and shaking for the rest of the night. The next morning we ate breakfast together and he left.

Several things happened that night. I allowed someone of whom I was afraid to become human to me, and as a result I reacted in a surprisingly human way to him. That caught him off guard. Apparently his scenario had not included a social visit, and it took him a few minutes to regain his sense of balance. By that time the vibes were all wrong for violence. Whatever had been motivating him was sidetracked, and he changed his mind.

Through the effects of prayer, meditation, training, and experience of lesser kinds of assault, I had been able to allow *a context for conversion* to emerge. I think Jesus was doing this in Gospel examples of self-defense. We catch a glimpse of this dynamic by observing how Jesus related to those who threatened him.

Jesus apparently did not find it effective to take away a person's ability to choose, even when his own welfare was the object of their choice. The scene in the garden of Gethsemane shows him dealing with personal assault. Never mind that he is about to be betrayed, that the soldiers are coming, already in sight, and armed to the teeth. He knows what to expect from soldiers. The worse agony is when his closest friends turn and run, abandon him. His front line of "defense" collapses. What does Jesus do? He could coerce them to stay. Guilt, physical restraint, public censure, and embarrassment would be effective. Instead, he lets them go.

Here is an awesome respect for the truth—the truth of the apostles' inability to be faithful. They simply are not ready. Perhaps Jesus lets them go because he knows that a coerced choice is no choice at all. To coerce them would block them from achieving the insight needed to choose to come back. Neither the kingdom nor truth can be taken by force. The nature of insight and truth requires that they be freely accepted. If the disciples are to choose to be faithful, they have to be allowed the freedom not to choose it. Jesus' action reflects his willingness to suffer the consequences of their free choice rather than to take away their ability to know the truth—even though that choice could involve evil.

But Jesus required more of people than a moment's choice. He showed himself willing to accompany the choice-making person by attempting to create a context for conversion. To create more inner availability to the truth, he fostered situations which evoked wonder and could reflect the consequences of people's actions back to them. He worked to create a context for conversion. His parables are models of this dynamic.

Jesus says, "If anyone wants to sue you and take your coat, give your cloak as well" (Matt. 5:40, NRSV). If someone takes one garment, the owner is advised to hand over the other. Why? In that climate, without both garments one will suffer from exposure to the elements. So, Jesus counsels, give away the cloak also. Let your adversary see in your nakedness the truth of what he is doing. Do something wonderful and open his eyes.

Jesus also says, "If anyone forces you to go one mile, go also the second mile" (Matt. 5:41, NRSV). This means walking the extra mile for an enemy, the Roman soldiers, who have the right to impress any Jew to carry their gear for one mile. For the first mile, the soldier has the power. But imagine the Jew refusing to lay down the burden after the first mile and walking on, freely, for the second mile. Who has the power after the first mile? Power relationships change. During the second mile, the Jew has the chance to work on the soldier, to help him come to insight about his actions, to help him see this Israelite as a person and not an object.

To have effective nonviolent defense, we must (1) radically respect the humanity of the person confronting us as an enemy, and (2) create a context for conversion. We blend these ingredients together through wisdom from our struggles to learn to love our enemies.

Our ability to facilitate disarmament in crisis situations, and thus gain real safety, can depend as much on our basic desire as on the assailant's intention. If I relate to an assailant out of a desire to win, to teach a lesson, or to get revenge, my behavior will reflect those desires. If my own safety is my only concern, I will act against the safety of the assailant, thus becoming threatening. The assailant is then put in a defensive position, and I lose any control of the interpersonal dynamic.

It is a hard journey from such desires to wanting the assailant's safety as well as my own. Yet this journey to my own personal disarmament is the basis of my ability to disarm someone else's will to hurt me. If I am in the process of disarming myself, I will begin to understand what is necessary to disarm another person. In the midst of the fear and vulnerability which I feel in the face of personal assault, something other than the will to destroy can surface, and my behavior can reflect that. I'll be freer to create a context for conversion because I know my self-preservation does not require the destruction of the other. Along the way, if I cannot yet love the persons who threaten me or desire their well-being, I can nurture that ability by remembering that, regardless of my feelings, these are loved persons.

The Gospels tell us that "God's love rains on the just and unjust alike" (based on Matt. 5:44-45). Whether the person confronting me is enemy or friend, that one is loved and valued by God; I need to be careful with what God values. Try as I might, I cannot escape the fact that the God whom Jesus revealed loves unconditionally. With the inbreaking of the kingdom, the favored-nation status ended. We are all loved with the same love originating in the same parent God. In nonviolence, I realize that this is a loved person, and I act out of a concern for our mutual safety. My actions are the consequence of my belief that as God's love is for me, so it is for everyone. Nonviolence is the manifestation of my commitment to and participation in that love.

When the assailant's safety is as important to me as my own, I can be free to disarm the crisis. Nonviolence primarily resides at this level of desire. Hence, internal personal disarmament work is crucial if I want to interact nonviolently with others in moments of crises.

As a victim, I have the power to stir up the assailants' ability to change their mind, or to encourage, however unconsciously, their desire to hurt me. Assailants are fully prepared for a hostile response or one of fear or panic. Sociologists say that most assailants work from a definite set of expectations about how the victim will respond. They need the victim to act as a victim to feed the polarization in the action-reaction interplay. A violent or hostile response, as well as a response of panic or helplessness, tends to reinforce the assailant's expectations, self-confidence, and sense of control. It also tends to increase cruelty within an already hostile person.

Assailants know how to play this game. They can handle what they are prepared for. Thus, using violent resistance to meet the situation limits oneself to the rules of the game as laid down by the assailant. Often one cannot reach a safe resolution within these confines.

While fear, panic, helplessness, and counterviolence can heighten hostility and cruelty, psychologists tell us that wonder tends to diffuse assailants. It seems to be nearly impossible for the human psyche to be in a state of wonder and a state of cruelty at the same time. Thus, introducing an element of wonder into the assault situation tends to be disarming—both to the person initiating the wonder and to the person responding to it.

Creating the context for conversion means doing something wonder-ful—nonthreatening, unexpected.

Wonder not only disarms; it tends to focus attention on whatever caused the wonder and places the recipient in a suggestive state of mind. When the human psyche focuses on what causes wonder, a desire to imitate tends to occur. Just as we have to cultivate within ourselves the desire for the assailant's safety, so we cultivate within the assailant a desire for our safety. "If you want to conquer another," said nonviolent strategist Richard Gregg, "do it not by outside resistance but by creating inside their own personality a strong new impulse that is incompatible with the previous tendency."

With the assailant temporarily thrown off balance by an unexpected, nonthreatening response on the part of the victim, it is possible to move the interaction to a different level. Gregg termed this dynamic *moral jujitsu*:

> The nonviolent [response] of the victim acts in the same way that the lack of physical opposition by the user of physical jujitsu does, causing the attacker to lose his moral balance. He suddenly and unexpectedly loses the moral support which the usual violent resistance of most victims would render him. . . . He feels insecure because of the novelty of the situation and his ignorance of how to handle it. He loses poise and self-confidence. . . . The user of nonviolent resistance, knowing what he is doing and having a more creative purpose, keeps his moral balance, using a different kind of leverage.

The art of jujitsu is based on the knowledge of balance and how to disturb it; so too is nonviolence. The resister short-circuits the flow of the assault by disarm-

---

*Richard B. Gregg, *The Power of Nonviolence* (Philadelphia: J. B. Lippincott Co.: 1935; revised editions, 1944, 1984), chapter 2.

ing responses and moves to take over the direction of
the encounter.

Here the *spirituality* behind nonviolence is crucial.
As important as techniques may be, the consciousness
from which they flow is even more so. The power of
nonviolence is in its ability to tap into the orientation of
creation toward wholeness. It requires activating the
dynamics mentioned above, such as the refusal to let
coercion inhibit achievement of the truth, radical respect for the other as a loved person, an orientation toward reconciliation rather than victory and domination,
and a valuing of the well-being of all.

If nonviolence is reduced to a technique and not au-
thentically rooted in these desires, it tends to be manip-
ulative. This can be catastrophic in an assault situation.
Successful use of nonviolence in the context of assault
requires that the victim act from an authentic desire for
common well-being. Such a desire can then be translat-
ed into building a common universe made up of a variety of small, seemingly insignificant actions.

Violence arms. That is its dynamic. Coercion creates
within the adversary the need for self-defense. Thus violence increases itself. The art of nonviolence is to
break the escalating cycle of threat and counterthreat,
to reverse its direction. The same mutual reinforcement
of response which can spiral into violent action can also
spiral into nonviolent action. Disarmament is impossible through violence. However, through nonviolence
we can firmly face an enemy and still allow love and
grace to so permeate the meeting that aggression becomes unnecessary and new choices become possible.

This 1983 essay is adapted from *The Universe Bends Toward Justice:
A Reader on Christian Nonviolence in the U.S.,* edited by Angie
O'Gorman, New Society Publications, 1990. Used by permission.

by Peggy Faw Gish

Neither Violent nor Victim

Maggie Harris, jogging through a city park at dusk, suddenly came face-to-face with a large man who had stepped out, blocking her path. She was terrified when he grabbed her arm. Just then she saw an old man walking his dog on a path across the park. She held back an impulse to call for help when she realized that the old man would likely get hurt if he tried to assist her. But this momentary change of focus toward the safety of the old man broke the paralysis of her fear.

With new courage Maggie jerked loose from the man's hold, grasped his arm, and said, "Let's go over here and talk." She led him to a less-secluded spot. After she expressed concern that he might be having some kind of trouble, he began to share about his plight and despair. Later he walked her home without harming her, thanking her for being his friend.

In another case, an older woman was walking down a city street carrying two large shopping bags. Two men came up behind her and overtook her on both sides. She knew what they were planning, but she was far from any residence or person she knew.

Before they got close enough to touch her or say anything, she turned and grinned at each of them, thrust her packages into their arms, and told them how relieved she felt now that they had come along. "I was rather nervous on this street," she said, "and these bags are so heavy. Would you help me?" Instinctively, the men took the packages, and the three walked along together as the woman cheerily thanked them and told them how kind they were to help.

These are situations that actually happened, not some theoretical gymnastics of the mind about "what if someone . . . ?" These real people, though frightened, did not let their fear or anger overcome them. Thus they were able to deal creatively in threatening situations. Out of an inner strength they probably didn't even know they possessed, they "turned the other cheek" (Matt. 5:39).

Here we need to stop and take a new look at the meaning of "turning the other cheek." It has been commonly understood as a stoic response, whereby the attacked persons grit their teeth and passively bear the abuse—even offering to take more!

I suspect this was not what Jesus really had in mind. Instead of passively fitting into the victim role, we are to do a *moral jujitsu* which completely turns around the whole situation. Instead of taking a weak, victim stance or retaliating out of anger or fear, we can respond in the power of love, truth, and a sense of justice. With this strength we can do the unexpected and the unimaginable, not fitting the expectations of the attacker. This catches the attacker off guard and breaks through the patterned role, opening the door for something new to happen.

For a Christian, this is a faithful response, coming out

of a foundation of inner strength and a respect for every person regardless of their behavior. It goes beyond a rational calculating of what would be the most practical or effective way to handle the situation. Attempts are made to restore a broken, distorted relationship into one of mutual respect, rather than to hurt the other or to get revenge. It is a response of nonviolent love.

The result is that the threatened person's response is less shackled by all the strategizing and speculating, by the impossible second guessing of "what if?" To an onlooker, such a response may even appear absurd or foolish. Yet, by coming from a sensitivity to the attackers' hurts and needs, this response is most likely to cut through their facade of power and expose their weakness and humanity.

For those most concerned about effectiveness, it is reassuring to know that this kind of moral jujitsu is highly effective when used as a strategy. There have been a wide variety of ways in which the nonviolent response has been carried out, ranging from serious conversing to using humor or absurdity.

Angie O'Gorman was awakened in the night by a man coming into her bedroom (story told on pages 120-129). She said the first thing that came into her head: "What time is it?" Her attacker became unnerved by her question and tried to look at his watch to answer her. After Angie inquired about his need for help and they talked briefly, she sent him downstairs to sleep. Here the mundane, almost absurd question broke the pattern. In other situations, humor, craziness, or even repulsive behavior disrupted the attack.

In a bus shelter in a deserted section of Cleveland, Joe and Peter were approached by two men with guns, demanding their money. Joe looked at the sky behind the attackers and yelled, "Wow, look! Here they come!" Both began to act crazy. The robbers got rattled and confused and ran away.

Mary was approached by two men on a dark city street. She quickly opened her handbag, pulled out some wadded-up tissues with scraps from an old lunch she had taken to work, and began retching and heaving, pretending to vomit. The men left, disgusted.

Two American college girls cavorting through Mexico took a carefree ramble through a city, through crowded streets and hovels, running, giggling, jostling. Their innocence and fearlessness protected them.

Coming home from a prayer meeting where they had sung an old hymn, "Under His wings I am safely abiding," an elderly woman was stopped by a man blocking her path. With confidence the woman blurted out, "You can't hurt me, I'm covered with his feathers!" She walked on unharmed.

Those who have experienced or studied these kinds of situations have attempted to describe the particular behavior that seemed helpful. Expressing strength in one's posture, voice, and body language; keeping good eye contact with the attacker; using deep breathing; consciously focusing on concern and love for the other (love casting out fear)—all these seemed to help the attacked person deal with the fear or reduce tension.

Would the response be different if the threat was directed toward someone close to you—your spouse, your mother, your child? Not significantly, though it could be more complicated. Our emotions could heighten, or we could rationalize that using violence was justified in order to save another person from harm.

Even when acting to protect another, a creative nonviolent response can completely turn around the tone or mode of relating. Yet we understand that there is no guarantee it will always work. Jesus never promised that followers of his way would not be persecuted or killed. But there is also no guarantee of effectiveness for a violent response to a threat.

Based on the experiences of the many who have used nonviolent defense, I believe that the chances of violence being carried out are much greater if one responds with violence or tries to physically overpower the other. The attacker feels more fearful and threatened and is more likely to use a weapon.

This happened to a sixty-two-year-old woman accosted by four unarmed men. She attempted to fend them off with a knife she carried for protection. The men took her knife and stabbed her seven times.

In our society we are told that we have to be tough to make it. But whole movements of people have found power in nonviolent confrontation to change oppressive conditions. Likewise, many individuals are trying the unthinkable, the unimaginable, turning the other cheek. They are finding it to be a response that neither harms the other nor puts themselves in a victim role.

Nonviolent confrontation is more effective than violence, and it can be carried out in love, courage, and strength. Such action is faithful to the vision of a people living out a life of reconciliation in a violent world.

Peggy Faw Gish works for the Appalachian Peace and Justice Network and is a member of an intentional Christian community at Athens, Ohio. Her essay is from the *Peace Studies Bulletin* of Manchester College. Used by permission.

by Art Gish

What If I Had Punched Him Back?

During the Vietnam War, as I was distributing anti-war leaflets at a high school, I was accosted by a twenty-year-old man. He cussed me out, then punched me in the face.

What should I have done?

Since he was bigger than I was, there was no point in me punching him back. That could have been a disaster for me.

I did remain nonviolent. Immediately after punching me, he broke down in tears; he told me that he was scheduled to leave for Vietnam the next week, and he definitely did not want to go. A long, intense conversation followed between the two of us.

What if I had been bigger than he, and I had punched him back? What would I have accomplished? I would have proved that I was bigger than he, which I would already have known.

By being nonviolent, by expressing openness and acceptance, I allowed the possibility of a breakthrough, of communication, and of new possibilities.

Last week I had a similar experience when I received a fantastic amount of hostility from another person. I tried to listen actively, to give "I" messages, and to reach him with peacemaking words, but each attempt seemed to fail. The hostility continued to pour out.

Yesterday I received from him the most humble letter I have ever received. His apology and recognition of his behavior were deeply moving for me.

What if I had become defensive and failed to try to reach him? What if I had punched him back?

Art Gish is an organic farmer, peace activist, author, and member of an intentional Christian community at Athens, Ohio. This article is from the *Peace Studies Bulletin* of Manchester College. Used by permission.

by
Lawrence
Hart

A Gesture of Peace

I am a Cheyenne Indian and a Mennonite Christian. I am also a Cheyenne Peace Chief,* committed to living a life of peace, no matter what the cost. Peace Chiefs are not to engage in quarrels or take sides in a dispute. Their task is to promote peace and harmony within the tribe as well as in the wider society.

"Even if your own son is killed right in front of you, you are to do nothing," one ancient saying instructs us. "If you see your mother, wife, or children being molested or harmed by anyone, do not take revenge. Take your pipe, go sit and smoke, and do nothing, for you are a Cheyenne Peace Chief," says another teaching.

This ethic comes to us from our ancient past. Like other tribes, we had developed sophisticated methods of conflict management and resolution.

---

*The chiefs of the Cheyenne, a Plains Indian tribe, are instructed to be peacemakers and are often called Peace Chiefs. The teachings of tribal hero Sweet Medicine guide the chiefs in being peaceful servants of the Cheyenne people. As European settlers invaded Cheyenne territory in the mid-1800s, Cheyenne chiefs worked for peace with U.S. soldiers, often with tragic results. Today, Cheyenne chiefs help to mediate tribal conflicts.

In 1968 the town of Cheyenne, Oklahoma, wanted to celebrate the centennial of the Battle of Washita. This so-called battle was actually a deliberate attack by Colonel George Armstrong Custer and his Seventh Cavalry on a peaceful village of Cheyenne governed by Peace Chief Black Kettle.

The townspeople invited the Cheyenne people to join in celebrating the hundred-year anniversary of this event. Initially we responded: "Celebrate? Celebrate the destruction of a peaceful village where women and children were killed? No, thank you!"

But the townspeople persisted in trying to convince us to join them. The Peace Chiefs thought about it. "How can we inform the well-intentioned townspeople that we cannot celebrate? If we do anything, we will commemorate, not celebrate. But how?"

The Peace Chiefs wrestled with this question and finally found an answer. The bones of one of the Cheyenne killed in that attack were on display in a museum. We decided to make the following proposal: We, the Cheyenne, will come and be part of the centennial activities if the townspeople allow us to bury the remains of our ancestor.

The townspeople were approached. They agreed to our conditions. A ceremony for this moment was planned; it was to be the last event of an entire day of celebration.

November 27, 1968, arrived and everything was in place. A tepee village had been set up at the actual site in preparation for one of the main events of the day, a reenactment of the attack. Hundreds of spectators and participants arrived.

Among those arriving were the grandsons of the Seventh Cavalry. They called themselves The Grand Army of the Republic, Grandsons of the Seventh Cavalry. They had come from California, and neither the townspeople nor the Cheyenne knew they were coming.

Dressed in authentic uniforms with real weapons and sabers, these grandsons of the Seventh joined in the mock attack. They approached the Cheyenne village in the same flanking movement used a hundred years before.

The scene looked so real to me. Hatred for these men began to rise within me. My feelings were intensified because my own children were in that village and would be shot down as rehearsed. I reminded myself that I was a Peace Chief, committed to nonviolence in action and thought. I remembered Peace Chief Black Kettle and the way he sought to live in peace. I resolved to do the same.

The attack took place. True to history, women and children were shot. Finally it was over, and we could proceed to the Black Kettle Museum. There we were to bury the hundred-year-old remains of a victim of that massacre.

We left the museum carrying a special bronze coffin, singing a Cheyenne song. Just like that day so long ago, it began to snow. As we passed through the crowd, a Cheyenne woman took off her blanket, a very beautiful Pendleton blanket, and draped it over the coffin. It was a gesture in keeping with our tradition.

Then, to my dismay, a command rang out: "Present arms!" I heard weapons being handled. The Grandsons of the Seventh were there. I didn't want them to be there, but they were. How dare they salute a victim of their forefathers' actions? I was not responding like a Peace Chief.

I was asked to be spokesperson for the Peace Chiefs, to explain the next part of the ceremony to the crowd. The blanket would be given away to someone who would be honored by the Cheyenne people. As I approached the podium, I knew the Peace Chiefs would be making a decision about who would receive the blanket. I told the crowd what was happening, and the chiefs made their decision.

I thought perhaps the chiefs would choose the governor or some other official. Instead, they asked me to announce that their choice was the commanding officer of the Grand Army of the Republic, Grandsons of the Seventh Cavalry. Captain Eric Gault stepped forward in sharp military fashion. The chiefs handed me the blanket. When the captain approached and came near me, he stopped, drew his sword, and saluted. As he replaced his sword, I asked him to turn around, and I draped the blanket over his shoulders.

One hundred years after the massacre of the Cheyenne by the Seventh Cavalry, the Peace Chiefs made a gesture of conciliation. The scene that followed is hard to describe. People broke down and cried. We cried on each other's shoulders—the grandsons of the Seventh and the grandsons of Black Kettle.

The captain responded to receiving the blanket by removing from his uniform a Garry Owen pin. That pin symbolized the bugle call for a charge, an attack—something Native Americans have heard so often.

Native Americans have no reason to celebrate events such as the Battle of the Washita or any of the many other incidents that illustrate the deliberate genocide or ethnocide of my people. Similarly, there is little or no cause for Native Americans to celebrate the quincentennial anniversary of the arrival of Christopher Columbus in North America.

But as a young Peace Chief in 1968, I learned the importance of gestures of conciliation from the elder Peace Chiefs. Taking my cue from those Peace Chief elders, I suggest that 1992 be a year of reconciliation— and every year after that!

Lawrence Hart, a Native American, lives in Clinton, Oklahoma. He is a Cheyenne Peace Chief and director of community services at the Cheyenne Cultural Center in Clinton. Hart serves on the Mennonite Central Committee U.S. Executive Board and is a member of the Koinonia (Okla.) Mennonite Church. This article is from the MCC packet "A Common History: Different Perspectives" and from *MCC Peace Office Newsletter* (March-April 1992). Used by permission of MCC and the author.

For more resources and dialogue (continued from page 143)

You may contact one or more of the following nondenominational peace education agencies:

Christian Peacemaker Teams,
   and Synapses
1821 W. Cullerton Ave.
Chicago, IL 60608

Clergy and Laity Concerned
P.O. Box 1987
Decatur, GA 30031

Evangelicals for Social Action
10 Lancaster Ave.
Wynnewood, PA 19096

The Fellowship of
   Reconciliation
Box 271
Nyack, NY 10960

Institute for Peace and justice
4144 Lindell, No. 122
St. Louis, MO 63108

New Call to Peacemaking
P.O. Box 500
Akron, PA 17501

Sojourners Peace Ministry
P.O. Box 29272
Washington, DC 20017

World Peacemakers
2025 Massachusetts Ave. NW
Washington, DC 20036

Christian Peace Resources

For serious study (from Herald Press except as noted)

Aukerman, Dale. *Darkening Valley* (1989, reprint of 1981).
_____ . *Reckoning with Apocalypse* (Crossroad, 1993).
Driedger, Leo, and Donald B. Kraybill. *Mennonite Peacemaking* (1994).
Durland, William R. *No King But Caesar?* 1975. A Catholic lawyer looks at Christian violence.
Enz, Jacob J. *The Christian and Warfare* (1972). Roots of pacifism in the Old Testament.
Friesen, Duane K. *Christian Peacemaking and International Conflict* (1986). Provides a realist pacifist perspective.
Gwyn, Douglas, G. Hunsinger, E. F. Roop, and J. H. Yoder, eds. *A Declaration on Peace: In God's People the World's Renewal Has Begun* (1990). Ecumenical dialogue.
Hershberger, Guy F. *War, Peace, and Nonresistance* (3d ed., 1969, 1991). Classic treatment of faith and history.
Hornus, Jean-Michel. *It Is Not Lawful for Me to Fight* (1980). Early Christian attitudes on war, violence, and the state.
Lasserre, Jean. *War and the Gospel* (1962). Analysis of Scriptures related to the ethical problem of war.
Lind, Millard C. *Yahweh Is a Warrior* (1980). Theology of warfare in ancient Israel.
Ramseyer, Robert L. *Mission and the Peace Witness* (1979).
Swartley, Willard M. *Slavery, Sabbath, War, and Women: Case Issues in Biblical Interpretation* (1983).
Trocmé, André. *Jesus and the Nonviolent Revolution* (1975).
Yoder, John H. *Nevertheless* (1992). On varieties of Pacifism.
_____ . *The Politics of Jesus* (Eerdmans, 1994).
_____ . *When War Is Unjust* (Augsburg Fortress, 1985).

For easy reading (from Herald Press except as noted)

Bainton, Roland H. *Christian Attitudes Toward War and Peace* (Abingdon Press, 1979). Classic on early church.

Barrett, Lois. *The Way God Fights* (1987). On the Bible.

Beachy, Duane. *Faith in a Nuclear Age* (1983).

Byler, Dennis. *Making War and Making Peace* (1989). Views since Constantine.

Drescher, John M. *Why I am a Conscientious Objector* (1982). For those facing military involvements.

Driver, John. *How Christians Made Peace with War* (1988). On the early church up to Augustine.

_____. *Kingdom Citizens* (1980). On Matthew 5–7.

Eller, V. *War and Peace from Genesis to Revelation* (1981).

Hostetler, Marian. *They Loved Their Enemies* (1988). Stories.

Kraybill, Donald B. *Facing Nuclear War* (1982).

_____. *The Upside-Down Kingdom* (1978, 1990). On wealth, war-making, status-seeking, religious exclusivism.

McSorley, Richard. *New Testament Basis of Peacemaking* (1985). Clear and sound interpretation by a Catholic.

Peachey, J. Lorne. *How to Teach Peace to Children* (1981).

Ruth-Heffelbower, Duane. *The Anabaptists Are Back! Making Peace in a Dangerous World* (1991). Stories.

Sider, Ronald J. *Christ and Violence* (1979).

Steiner, Susan Clemmer. *Joining the Army That Sheds No Blood* (1982). Biblical pacifism, written for teens.

Stoner, John K., and Lois Barrett. *Letters to American Christians* (1989). On evangelicalism and militarism.

Wenger, J. C. *The Way of Peace* (1977). A brief treatment.

For children of all ages (from Herald Press)

Bauman, Elizabeth H. *Coals of Fire* (1954). Stories.

Dyck, Peter J. *The Great Shalom* (1990). *Shalom at Last* (1992). Animals work with the farmer to save the forest.

Eitzen, Ruth and Allan. *The White Feather* (1987). Story.

Meyer, Mary Clemens. *Walking with Jesus* (1992). Stories.

Moore, Ruth Nulton. *The Christmas Surprise* (1989). *Distant Thunder* (1991). Peacemaking Moravians in wartime.

(For more resources, see page 141)

The Author

John H. Yoder is professor of theology at the University of Notre Dame (Ind.). He has also taught at the Associated Mennonite Biblical Seminaries of Elkhart (Indiana), the University of Strasbourg, the Instituto Superior Evangelico of Buenos Aires, and in courses at Berkeley, Vancouver, and Melbourne. He received the doctor of theology degree from the University of Basel.

Prior to 1965 Yoder served in Europe and North America with the relief and mission agencies of the Mennonite churches. He also represented his denomination in interchurch conversations on matters of evangelism and social ethics.

Other writings by Yoder deal with issues of war and peace, Reformation history, ethics, missionary methods, church renewal, and the ecumenical movement.

Born at Smithville, Ohio, John is married to Anne Marie Guth. They are the parents of six living children and are members of Prairie Street Mennonite Church, Elkhart, Indiana.